READING AND TRAINING

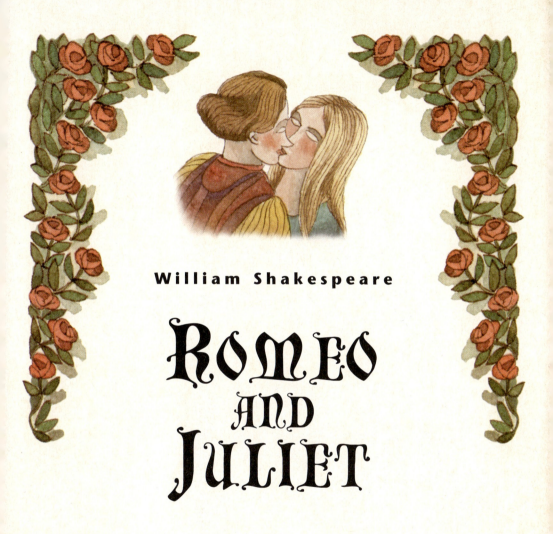

William Shakespeare

Romeo and Juliet

Text adaptation, notes and activities
by Derek Sellen

Dossier sections written by Gina D. B. Clemen
Editors: Rebecca Raynes, Elvira Poggi Repetto
Design: Nadia Maestri
Illustrations: Giovanni Manna

© Cideb Editrice S.r.l.
Rapallo – Italy 1997

ISBN 3-425-03097-3

© 1999 Verlag Moritz Diesterweg GmbH & Co., Frankfurt am Main.
Alle Rechte vorbehalten. Das Werk und seine Teile sind urheberrechtlich geschützt. Jede Verwertung in anderen als den gesetzlich zugelassenen Fällen bedarf deshalb der vorherigen schriftlichen Einwilligung des Verlages

Druck und Verarbeitung: Westermann, Braunschweig
Printed in Germany

Contents

Shakespeare's Life	5
Shakespeare and *Romeo and Juliet*	8
Summary	10
Dramatis Personae	12

PART ONE — The Montagues and the Capulets — 13

    ACTIVITIES — 21
1. Comprehension and Opinion
2. Grammar and Vocabulary – *using adjectives*
3. Grammar – *'too' with an adjective*
4. Vocabulary – *families*
5. Listening – *the Queen of the Fairies*
6. Writing – *the Verona Times*

PART TWO — The Garden of the Capulets — 28

    ACTIVITIES — 35
1. Comprehension and Opinion
2. Grammar – *use of adverbs*
3. Vocabulary – *love and marriage*
4. Grammar – *Past Simple and Past Continuous*
5. Listening – *the Party*
6. Writing – *choosing*

A Walk through Verona — 42

PART THREE — The Prince of Cats — 46

    ACTIVITIES — 51
1. Comprehension and Opinion
2. Vocabulary – *animals and character*
3. Grammar – *the Present Perfect*
4. Listening – *the Nurse and Juliet*
5. Writing – *a summary*

PART FOUR	**Fortune's Fool**	58
	ACTIVITIES	64

   1. Comprehension and Opinion
   2. Vocabulary – *word formation*
   3. Grammar – *already, still and yet*
   4. Listening – *four Zodiac signs*
   5. Writing – *horoscopes*
   6. Writing – *a bad luck story*

   Life in Renaissance Verona — 69

PART FIVE	**My Lady's Dead!**	72
	ACTIVITIES	78

   1. Comprehension and Opinion
   2. Grammar – *ought to*
   3. Opinion and Writing – *parents and children*
   4. Grammar – *Past Perfect versus Past Simple*
   5. Listening – *true and false*
   6. Writing – *the Verona Times*

PART SIX	**With a Kiss, I Die**	84
	ACTIVITIES	90

   1. Comprehension and Opinion
   2. Grammar – *Past Simple Passive*
   3. Writing – *the Verona Times*
   4. Listening – *lines from Shakespeare*
   5. Opinion – *characters in the play*
   6. Writing – *all the Romeos and all the Juliets*

   Juliet through the Centuries — 95

   Playscript — 97

This story is recorded in full on the cassette.

Introduction

Shakespeare's Life

William Shakespeare was born in Stratford-upon-Avon in the English Midlands on
St. George's Day, April 23rd, 1564. (St. George is the patron saint of England.)
He was the third child of John Shakespeare, a glove-maker,[1] who was an
important man in the town, and Mary Arden. He went to Stratford Grammar
School, where he received a good education, but he did not go to university.
In 1582, when he was only eighteen, he married Anne Hathaway. They had three
children – Hamnet, a boy who died when he was only eleven years old, Susanna
and Judith. As far as we know, they were happily married. When he died he left
his 'second-best bed' to his wife in his will.[2] Perhaps it was their marriage bed.
Very little is known about Shakespeare's later life. There is a legend that he had to
leave Stratford because he was caught stealing a deer.[3]

1. **glove-maker** : someone who makes gloves.
2. **will** : testament, a document written before someone dies.
3. **deer** :

Introduction

Shakespeare was born in this house in Stratford-upon-Avon.

Shakespeare went to London and became involved [1] in the world of the theatre. Drama then was as important a part of life as television is for us. All classes of society enjoyed the plays by Shakespeare and other Elizabethan dramatists.
Did you know that in Shakespeare's theatre, boys played the parts of women? Juliet, Cleopatra, Desdemona and Lady Macbeth were all played by young men whose voices had not broken. Actresses were not allowed on the English stage until late in the following century.
Shakespeare quickly became very popular as a writer. One of his rivals called him a 'crow' [2] who had stolen the 'feathers' [3] of the other writers.

1. **involved** : interested.
2. **crow** : a black bird.
3. **feathers** :

Introduction

His friend, Ben Jonson, wrote that he was 'honest, open and free'. Another writer said that he was 'handsome', 'well-shaped' and had a 'pleasant smooth wit'. [1] Apart from the plays, he also wrote a collection of Sonnets. Many of these poems are written to a 'Dark Lady', but nobody can discover her identity.
We do not know very much about Shakespeare's personal life but plays such as *Romeo and Juliet* show that he was very interested in the theme of passionate love. When Shakespeare died – on his birthday in 1616 – he was buried in Stratford. There are four lines written on his tombstone, including these:

> Blessed [2] is the man who spares [3] these stones
> And cursed [4] is the man who moves my bones.

Perhaps these lines show that Shakespeare did not want us to know about his personal life. Instead, he has left us his poems and plays.

Ben Jonson.

1. **wit** : intelligent humour.
2. **blessed** : happy, lucky.
3. **spares** : does not touch.
4. **cursed** : unlucky, unhappy.

Shakespeare and Romeo and Juliet

Shakespeare wrote *Romeo and Juliet* in the middle of the 1590's. Elizabeth the First was Queen of England. During her reign, [1] the country had made great progress in many different areas – travelling by sea, exploration, war, music, architecture, drama and poetry. England had become a major power in Europe and had defeated the Spanish Armada in 1588 when Philip the Second had attempted to invade the country.

In all the arts, there was great influence from Italy. The Renaissance had begun in Italy and the English were very enthusiastic about Italian culture. Chaucer, the first important English poet, respected Dante as the greatest European poet. The most popular form of love poetry, the Sonnet, was 'borrowed' [2] from Italian writers. Many of Shakespeare's plays are located in Italy and based on Italian stories. For the English, Italy was the country of passion, vendettas, murder, suicide and deep emotion. When Shakespeare wanted to write a tragedy of love and death, he chose an Italian story.

The legend of Romeo and Juliet had been very popular in England for a long time.

1. **reign** [reɪn] : the period when a king or queen has power.
2. **borrowed** : taken.

Introduction

Shakespeare took the story, changed some of the details and made it into a great play with characters which live in the memory. He changed the age of Juliet; in his play, she is only thirteen years old. It was possible to get married at twelve or thirteen but most people in Elizabethan society waited until later. 'Arranged marriages' were normal. In other words, the family decided who their sons and daughters should marry. There are many stories about the conflict between the wishes [1] of the parents and the romantic feelings of their children.

Romeo and Juliet has the reputation of being the perfect love story. But it is not only about love. It is also about hate between the Montagues and the Capulets. It ends, not in marriage, but in death. The lovers are very young. Romeo changes his mind easily; at the beginning of the play, he loves Rosaline, not Juliet. He often acts without thinking and he kills two people. Juliet also changes her mind. She thinks she is too young to get married but when she sees Romeo...!!!

1. **wishes** : desires.

The story of Romeo and Juliet has lived until the present day. Other writers and musical composers have produced their own interpretations of the old, old story. But Shakespeare was the first one to make a great work of dramatic art from the story of the 'star-crossed [1] lovers' who lived in Renaissance Verona.

SUMMARY

In the beautiful city of Verona, there are two families who hate each other. When Romeo from the Montagues and Juliet from the Capulets fall in love, it creates problems for everybody. Friar Lawrence, kind and optimistic, tries to help the young lovers. But there are other people in Verona, such as Tybalt, the 'Prince of Cats', who want to destroy the peace of the city. 'True Love' has to fight to survive...

1. **star-crossed** : unlucky.

ACTIVITIES

1 How much do you remember about Shakespeare? Complete the summary by choosing the correct words.

William Shakespeare was born in *1564 / 1664 / 1774*. He was the *fourth / first / third* child of John Shakespeare, a *glove-maker / painter / doctor*. When he was eighteen he married Anne Hathaway and they had *three / four / two* children.

A *lot / some / only a little* is known about Shakespeare's life. There is a legend that he had to leave Stratford because he was caught stealing a *deer / cow / dog*. He went to *Leeds / Liverpool / London* and became involved in the theatre.

He became very popular as an *actor / writer / singer* and one of his rivals accused him of *copying / helping / criticizing* other writers.

As well as his plays he wrote a collection of *poems / novels / reviews*. Many of these were written to a 'Dark Lady'.

Shakespeare died on *Christmas Day / his wedding anniversary / his birthday* in 1616 and he was buried in *London / Stratford / Stirling*.

2 Are these sentences true (T) or false (F)? Correct the false ones.

		T	F
a.	*Romeo and Juliet* was written in the middle of the 1950's.	☐	☐
b.	In the arts, there was great influence from Italy.	☐	☐
c.	Dante respected Chaucer as the greatest European poet.	☐	☐
d.	All of Shakespeare's plays are located in Italy.	☐	☐
e.	In England the people had never heard of the legend of Romeo and Juliet.	☐	☐
f.	Shakespeare changed some of the details for his version.	☐	☐
g.	In his play Juliet is only seventeen years old.	☐	☐
h.	Arranged marriages were normal in Elizabethan society.	☐	☐
i.	*Romeo and Juliet* is about love and hate.	☐	☐
j.	The story ends happily.	☐	☐

....
....
....

DRAMATIS PERSONAE

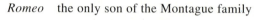

Romeo	the only son of the Montague family
Juliet	the only daughter of the Capulet family
The Prince	the governor of Verona
Lord Capulet	Juliet's father
Lady Capulet	Juliet's mother
Lord Montague	Romeo's father
Lady Montague	Romeo's mother
Benvolio	Romeo's cousin
Tybalt	Juliet's cousin
Mercutio	Romeo's friend
Paris	a friend of the Prince and of the Capulets
The Nurse	
Friar Lawrence	
Friar John	
Balthasar	Romeo's servant
Servants	

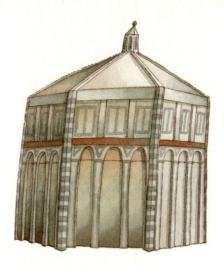

PART ONE

The Montagues and the Capulets

In the beautiful city of Verona, there were two families – the Montagues and the Capulets. They hated each other. They had hated each other for hundreds of years.

One day, two servants of the house of Capulet were walking in the streets.

'If I meet any man or woman from the house of Montague, I'll push them out of the way,' said Sampson.

'No, you'll run away,' laughed his friend, Gregory.

'Don't worry about that,' said Sampson. 'I will stand and fight.'

Just then, two servants from the house of Montague came into the same street.

Romeo and Juliet

Sampson took out his sword [1] and bit [2] his thumb [3] at them. This was a great insult. The two groups of servants began to fight.

'The Montagues are better than the Capulets,' shouted the servants of the Montagues.

'Our masters, the Capulets, are better,' shouted the servants of the Capulets.

Then Benvolio, a member of the Montague family, arrived. He tried to make peace.

'Stop, fools! Put away your swords.'

But no-one listened to him. The servants continued fighting and Benvolio took out his sword to stop them. Then Tybalt arrived. He was a Capulet, the most dangerous member of the family. He loved fighting.

'Benvolio, you have drawn [4] your sword. Now you must fight with me. Look at your death!'

'I am only trying to separate these fools,' replied Benvolio. 'Put away your sword or use it to help me keep the peace.'

'Peace!' snarled [5] Tybalt. 'I hate the word. I hate all Montagues and I hate you!'

1. **sword** [sɔːd] :
2. **bit** : past tense of 'to bite'.
3. **thumb** : the largest finger, 'biting your thumb' was a great insult in this period of history.
4. **drawn your sword** : (to draw-drew-drawn) taken out your sword.
5. **snarled** : said in a fierce angry way.

PART ONE

With those words, Tybalt attacked Benvolio with his sword.

Then Lord and Lady Capulet arrived. Lord Capulet was old but he wanted to fight too. 'Bring me my sword,' he shouted.

'You are too old to fight,' said Lady Capulet. 'You don't need a sword, you need a crutch.' [1]

Then Lord and Lady Montague arrived. Lord Montague was swinging [2] his sword although his wife tried to stop him.

More and more people came. Soon everyone was fighting. It was very dangerous.

At last, the Prince of Verona arrived. He was very angry.

'Stop fighting! I want peace in my city! Drop your weapons or you will all die! This is the third time that your families have been fighting in the streets.

'Lord Capulet and Lord Montague, you are old but you are not wise. You must promise not to fight. Lord Capulet, come with me now. We must talk. Lord Montague, come to see me this afternoon. If your two families fight again, you will both die!'

Everyone went away except the Montagues. The fight was over.

'How did it begin?' Lord Montague asked Benvolio.

'The servants were fighting. I drew my sword to stop them. Then Tybalt arrived. He began fighting with me. Soon everyone was involved.' [3]

1. **a crutch** : something to help an old person to walk.
2. **swinging** : moving violently.
3. **involved** : part of the fight.

Romeo and Juliet

'Where is my son, Romeo? Is he safe?' asked Lady Montague. 'I saw him this morning, an hour before the sunrise,' replied Benvolio. 'He was walking alone in the fields. He saw me but he didn't want my company. He went into the forest.'

Lord Montague nodded. 'People have often seen him there in the morning. He cries. Then he comes home and locks [1] himself in his room. He shuts out the daylight and spends all his time alone in the dark. Something is wrong.'

'Have you questioned him?'

'Yes, but he gives no answer.'

'But look, he is coming now,' said Benvolio. 'I will ask him about his problems.'

'I hope he will answer you. We will leave you to speak privately,' said Lord Montague.

Romeo was on his way back from the forest to the city.

'Good morning, cousin,' said Benvolio.

'It is a sad morning,' replied Romeo.

'Why? Why are your days sad and long?'

'I am...'

'In love?'

---

1. **locks** : shuts his door with a key.

PART ONE

'Out...'

'Out of love?'

'Out of my lady's favour. I love her but she does not love me. Love is a terrible thing, Benvolio. I love and I hate. Love comes from nothing. It is heavy and light, serious and foolish, hot and cold, sick and healthy. Are you laughing at me?'

'No, I am sad because you are sad.'

'Love is a madness [1]. Goodbye, cousin.'

'Tell me, who do you love?'

'I love a woman.'

'I know that. But who?'

'I love sweet Rosaline. She is beautiful, intelligent and good. But she does not love me.'

'Forget her. There are many other girls.'

'No, I can never forget her.'

Lord Capulet decided to have a party.

'I will invite all the important people from Verona. But not the Montagues.'

He wanted his daughter, Juliet, to meet Paris, a lord from Verona, the friend of the Prince. He hoped she would marry Paris in the future. He called for his servant.

'Here is a list of names. Go and invite the guests.'

The servant met Romeo and Benvolio in the street. He did not know that they were Montagues. 'Can you help me?' he asked. 'I can't read the names on this piece of paper.'

---

1. **madness** : (G.) Wahnsinn.

Romeo and Juliet

'Look, Romeo. Rosaline will be at the party.'

'I have an idea,' said Romeo suddenly.

Meanwhile,[1] Lady Capulet was talking to Juliet, her thirteen year-old daughter. Juliet had an old nurse[2] who looked after her.

'You will meet Paris at the party,' Lady Capulet told Juliet. 'Perhaps you will marry him one day.'

'Mother, I am too young to get married,' replied Juliet.

'I would love to see my little Juliet married,' said the Nurse. 'You will have happy days and happy nights.'

1. **Meanwhile** : at the same time.
2. **nurse** : a woman employed to look after the children.

ACTIVITIES

Comprehension and Opinion

1 **What happened in Part One?**

  a. What are the names of the two families?
  b. Did Benvolio and Tybalt want the same thing?
  c. Why was the Prince angry?
  d. Why was Romeo unhappy?
  e. How did Romeo and Benvolio get information about the party?
  f. Why did Lord and Lady Capulet want Juliet to meet Paris?

What do you think?

What will happen next? What is Romeo's idea?

Using Adjectives

2 **a.** **Can you remember the adjectives which are used in the story? Fill these gaps.**

  a. In the _ _ _ _ _ _ _ _ _ city of Verona, there were two families.
  b. Tybalt was the most _ _ _ _ _ _ _ _ _ member of the Capulet family.
  c. The Prince was very _ _ _ _ _ _ .
  d. 'You are _ _ _ but you are not _ _ _ _ .'
  e. 'Why are your days _ _ _ and _ _ _ _ _ ?'
  f. 'Rosaline is _ _ _ _ _ _ _ _ _ _ , _ _ _ _ _ _ _ _ _ _ _ _ and _ _ _ _ .'
  g. 'You will have _ _ _ _ _ days and _ _ _ _ _ nights.'

ACTIVITIES

b. Make a chain ¹ of adjectives. Use the last letter to begin the next adjective.

For example:
dangerous-**s**-stupid-**d**-difficult-**t**-tall-**l**-loud-**d**-dangerous

How many words can you include in your chain?

c. Opposites

Romeo uses adjectives with opposite meanings to describe love: 'Love is heavy and light, serious and foolish, hot and cold, sick and healthy.' Look at these adjectives:

> beautiful   cruel   fat   friendly   hard-working
> happy   intelligent   kind   lazy   modest   poor
> proud   rich   sad   short   stupid   tall
> terrible   thin   ugly   unfriendly   wonderful

Beautiful and *ugly* are opposites.
There are ten more pairs of opposites in the box. What are they?

1. beautiful / ugly
2. ....
3. ....
4. ....
5. ....
6. ....
7. ....
8. ....
9. ....
10. ....
11. ....

1. chain :

ACTIVITIES

d. **Synonyms**

Sometimes there are adjectives which have the same or similar meanings. These are called *synonyms*. Here are six words:

happy	sad	rich	beautiful	wonderful	thin

Which words in the box below have similar meanings? There are three synonyms for each word above. Fill in the table.

> affluent   attractive   depressed   ecstatic
> slim   excellent   fantastic   great   glad
> handsome   joyful   miserable   pretty   prosperous
> skinny   slender   unhappy   wealthy

N.B. There are often special uses for adjectives:

For example:
prosperous and **affluent** are formal words.
Skinny is negative but **slim** is positive.
Handsome is usually used for men or boys.
Ecstatic is stronger than **happy**.

ACTIVITIES

'Too' with an Adjective

3 In the story, Juliet says: 'I am too young to get married.' Lady Capulet says: 'You are too old to fight.'
How many more sentences can you make? Use: ' ...too...to...'
Use the words below.

a.	lazy	to carry
b.	tired	to drive a car
c.	fat	to go shopping
d.	young	to dance
e.	cold	to study
f.	ill	to go to bed
g.	unhappy	to wear this dress
h.	late	to pass the test
i.	early	to go to the beach
j.	heavy	to eat dinner
k.	stupid	to learn English
l.	poor	to make a mistake
m.	intelligent	to play football

For example:
It's too late to go shopping.
She's too tired to study.
He's too lazy to carry this suitcase.

Who can make the most sentences?

Now practise questions and answers with a friend:
Why don't you go shopping? It's too late.
Why don't you study? I'm too tired.

ACTIVITIES

Families

4 Complete these words. Each word is the name of a member of a family.

a. Romeo is Lord Montague's   s _ _
b. My father's sister is my   a _ _
c. Juliet is Lady Capulet's   d _ _ _ _ t e r
d. Lord Montague is Romeo's   f _ _ _ _
e. Benvolio is Romeo's   _ o u s i n
f. Lady Capulet is Juliet's   m _ _ _ _
g. Romeo is an only child. He has no   b r _ _ _ _ _ s
h. He has no   s _ _ _ _ _
i. Romeo has two   p a r _ _ _
j. Lady Capulet is Lord Capulet's   w _ _ _
k. He is her   h _ _ _ _ _ _
l. My father's brother is my   u _ _ _
m. My mother's mother is my   grand _ _ _ _ _
n. My sister's son is my   n _ _ _ _ _

Now read DOWN from the letter 's' in the first line.
Put the letters in these spaces:

S _ _ _ - _ _ _ _ _ _ _   _ _ V _ R S

This is Shakespeare's description of Romeo and Juliet. The first word means 'unlucky'.

A C T I V I T I E S

The Queen of the Fairies [1]

5 a. Listen to Part One of *Romeo and Juliet* on the cassette.
After the bells, you will hear Romeo and his friend talking. His friend's name is Mercutio. He loves making jokes. [2] He has a lot of imagination.

b. Listen a second time. Put the words from the box in the right places in the script.

> dangerous   dreams   killing   kisses   late   love
> name   quiet   sleeping   small   tired   unhappy

Mercutio: What's the matter, Romeo? Why are you so .... tonight?

Romeo: I am .... I am in love.

Mercutio: Don't be stupid. We'll be .... for the party. There will be lots of beautiful girls there.

Romeo: I am very .... Last night, I dreamt about sweet Rosaline. I didn't sleep well.

Mercutio: Ah! The Queen of the Fairies has been with you.
Her .... is Queen Mab.
She is very ....
She rides over our noses while we are ....
She gives us our ....
When she visits them, girls dream about ....
Soldiers [3] dream about ....
Lovers dream about ....
She is very .... She can change our lives.

1. **fairies** : plural of fairy, a small magical creature with wings.
2. **making jokes** : saying funny things.
3. **soldiers** [soʊldʒəz] : military men, men who fight.

ACTIVITIES

The Verona Times

6 A newspaper reporter from *The Verona Times* interviewed a citizen [1] from Verona. He asked these questions:

- Did you see the fight?
  Yes, I was very afraid.
- Did you hear the Prince?
  Yes, he is a good man. He was right. The fighting is dangerous. It must stop.
- Did you hear Lord Capulet and Lord Montague? What did they say?
  They said they will never fight again.

The questions are about the past. They use 'did...'
Did you see...? Did you hear...? What did they say...?
Here are three other citizens of Verona:

a friend of the Montagues

a friend of the Capulets

an old lady of Verona

Write an interview between a reporter and each citizen. Write three questions and three answers about what happened between the Capulets and the Montagues.

1. **citizen** : (G.) Bürger.

PART TWO

The Garden of the Capulets

Romeo went to the party with Benvolio and his friend, Mercutio. They were all wearing masks. It was very dangerous for the Montagues and their friends to go to a party in the house of the Capulets.

'I cannot wait ¹ to see fair ² Rosaline,' said Romeo as they approached ³ the house.

Lord Capulet welcomed them. 'Come in, gentlemen. Dance and drink and eat. Enjoy yourselves.' He did not recognise the son of his enemy, Lord Montague.

He spoke to all the guests. 'Now, girls, dance to the music. When I was younger, I whispered sweet things in the ears of the

---

1. **I cannot wait** : I am very excited.
2. **fair** : beautiful.
3. **approached** : came near.

PART TWO

ladies. But now I am old. My dancing days are finished. I will sit here with the old people and talk about the past.'

As they went into the house, Romeo saw Juliet for the first time.

He forgot Rosaline! He fell in love!

'Who is that lady?' asked Romeo. 'She is more beautiful than the moon. She is like a bright jewel [1] in the darkness. She is like a dove [2] among crows. I have never loved until now.'

But Tybalt recognised Romeo's voice. 'It is a Montague. Bring me my sword. It is a great insult for a Montague to come here to laugh at our party. I will kill him.'

'What's the matter, Tybalt?' asked Lord Capulet.

'That man in the mask is a Montague, uncle.'

'Be calm, Tybalt. Is it Romeo? He has a good reputation in Verona. This is a party. I want no trouble in my house. Let him enjoy himself.'

'No, uncle. He is our enemy.'

'Don't be cheeky, [3] young man. I am the master in this house.

---

1. **jewel** : for example, a diamond or a pearl.
2. **dove** : a beautiful white bird.
3. **cheeky** : rude, not polite.

Romeo and Juliet

You must do as I say.'

Tybalt did not agree but he did not want to make Lord Capulet angry. 'I will leave the party. I cannot stay here with a Montague in the room. But I will not forget. Romeo will have a good time tonight but tomorrow he will pay!'

Romeo went to Juliet and talked to her. He did not know who she was. He took her hand gently [1] in his.

'My lips are ready to kiss you,' he said softly.

'I do not know you,' protested Juliet.

'I must kiss you,' insisted Romeo.

'Here I am,' said Juliet. 'My lips are here.'

Romeo kissed Juliet. He kissed her a second time.

Then the Nurse came to take Juliet to her mother.

'That is Juliet. She is a Capulet,' the Nurse told Romeo.

Romeo was very surprised and upset. [2] He was in love with the daughter of the enemy of his family.

'Quickly, let's go,' said Benvolio. 'It is dangerous here.'

Juliet asked the Nurse, 'Who is that young man?'

'That is Romeo. He is a Montague.'

Juliet was also very surprised and upset. She was in love with the son of the enemy of her family. 'We can never get married,' she thought.

After they left the party, Mercutio and Benvolio looked for Romeo.

'Look! He is there in the shadows. [3] What is he doing?' said Mercutio.

1. **gently** : carefully.
2. **upset** : sad, confused.
3. **shadows** : dark places without light.

PART TWO

'He is jumping the wall. He is going into the garden of the Capulets.'

Mercutio called out. 'Romeo! Madman! Lover! He is going to look for Rosaline.'

'Quiet! You will make him angry,' said Benvolio. 'His love is blind.'

Mercutio laughed. 'Good night, Romeo. He is probably sitting under a tree, dreaming about that girl. He is mad.'

Mercutio and Benvolio went home. The night was silent.

In the dark garden, Romeo suddenly saw a light. Juliet was standing on her balcony. 'She is beautiful,' he thought. 'Her eyes are stars. They give light to the night. Her glove [1] touches her cheek [2] – I would like to be her glove!'

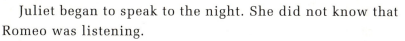

Juliet began to speak to the night. She did not know that Romeo was listening.

'Ah, Romeo,' she sighed. [3]

'Speak again, angel,' he whispered. [4]

'O Romeo, Romeo! Why is your name Romeo?

---

1. **glove** : you wear this on your hand.
2. **cheek** : the side of the face.
3. **sighed** [saɪd] : breathed heavily.
4. **whispered** : said very quietly.

Romeo and Juliet

Let's change our names. Then we can love.
Forget that you are a Montague.
Or, if you love me, I will not be a Capulet.
Montague and Capulet are only names.
A rose can have any name. It always smells sweet.'
Romeo called out. [1] 'I will change my name for you.'
'Who's there?' asked Juliet. 'Who is listening in the middle of the night?'
'I will not tell you my name because it is your enemy.'
'I know your voice. Are you Romeo? But how did you get over the garden wall?'
'Love gave me wings. [2] No walls can shut out [3] love.'
'If my family find you, they will murder you.'
'The night hides me. I am safe. Love has sent me here to you.'
Romeo and Juliet talked together. Romeo knew Juliet's secret – she loved him. They decided to get married secretly.
'Will you be true?' [4] asked Juliet.
'Yes, my darling,' replied Romeo. 'I promise by the moon.'
'But the moon changes. Will your love change?'
'Never. I will always love you. Do you love me?'
'I told the night that I loved you and you heard me. But I wish I had been silent.'

1. **called out** : spoke loudly.
2. **wings** :
3. **shut out** : (G.) aussperren.
4. **true** : faithful, loyal.

Romeo and Juliet

'Have you changed your mind?'

'No, my love is as deep as the sea. But I must go. The Nurse is calling. Good night, Romeo.'

'Good night, Juliet.'

The Nurse called: 'Juliet! Juliet!'

'I'm coming, Nurse. Good night.'

'Good night.'

'It is very sad and very sweet to say good night. But tomorrow, we will be married.'

ACTIVITIES

Comprehension and Opinion

1 **What happened in Part Two?**

    a. Why were Romeo and his friends wearing masks?
    b. What happened when Romeo saw Juliet?
    c. What did Romeo and Juliet do?
    d. How did Romeo enter the garden?
    e. Where was Juliet?
    f. What did Romeo and Juliet decide to do?

What do you think?

Will Romeo and Juliet get married?
Will they be happy? Do they really love each other?

Use of Adverbs

2 **We use adverbs to describe actions. They usually end in '-ly'.**

For example:
They will get married secretly.

Adjectives ending in '-ic' usually add '-ally'.
For example:
How did Mercutio talk about Romeo? Sarcastically.

A few adverbs do not end in '-ly'.
For example:
He ran fast. They worked hard.

ACTIVITIES

Complete the sentences below with suitable adverbs from the box:

> angrily   anxiously   beautifully   comically
> immediately   kindly   loudly   lovingly
> passionately   sadly   stupidly   violently

a. Romeo fell in love with Juliet ....

b. The Prince spoke ....

c. Benvolio behaved ....

d. Tybalt fought ....

e. The Nurse called ....

f. Juliet thought about Romeo ....

g. The servants behaved ....

h. Romeo and Juliet loved each other ....

i. At the party, Juliet danced ....

j. Lady Montague asked about Romeo ....

A C T I V I T I E S

Love and Marriage

3 In Shakespeare's play, Juliet says good night to Romeo with these words:

1 2 3 4 5 6 7   5 8   8 9 10 11
_ _ _ _ _ _ _   _ _   _ _ _ _

8 12 13 13 4   8 14 3 3 14 12
_ _ _ _ _   _ _ _ _ _ _

Each number represents a letter of the alphabet.
If you can find the words in the gaps below, you will be able to know what Juliet said.

For example:
The answer for number **1** is 'RING'.
Therefore, 3 = R 5 = I 6 = N 7 = G

1. A married woman wears this on her finger: 3 5 6 7
2. When people get married there is a: 12 13 **D D** 5 6 7
3. The woman who gets married is the: **B** 3 5 **D** 13
4. The man who gets married is the: **B** 3 5 **D** 13 7 3 14 14 **M**
5. They usually get married in a: 10 11 9 3 10 11
6. They are married in church by a: 1 3 5 13 8 4
7. Everybody hopes the couple will be: 11 2 1 1 **Y**
8. But sometimes marriages end in: **D** 5 **V** 14 3 10 13
9. Romeo and Juliet will marry: 8 13 10 3 13 4 **L Y**
10. Sometimes people have a broken: 11 13 2 3 4
11. Romeo and Juliet were in: **L** 14 **V** 13
12. They fell in love at first: 8 5 **G** 11 4
13. Rosaline was Romeo's first: **G** 5 3 **L F** 3 5 13 6 **D**

Do you understand Juliet's words? If not, ask your teacher or a friend who knows good English to explain them to you.

ACTIVITIES

Past Simple and Past Continuous

4 Look at this sentence:
While Romeo was looking for Rosaline, he saw Juliet.

The first action continued for a long time:
'Romeo was looking...' (Past Continuous)
The second action happened suddenly, during this time:
'he saw...' (Past Simple)

Now put the verbs in these sentences in the Past Continuous (was/were -ing) or Past Simple form. Remember that some verbs have an irregular past form (e.g. 'see' - 'saw')

a. While Benvolio (try) to stop the fight, Tybalt (arrive).
b. The Prince (see) that everybody (fight).
c. Benvolio (walk) near the forest when he (meet) Romeo.
d. The Nurse (help) Juliet when her mother (come) into the room.
e. While Romeo and Juliet (kiss), the Nurse (see) them.
f. Tybalt (recognise) Romeo's voice while he (talk).
g. While Romeo (stand) in the garden, Juliet (begin) to speak.
h. While Juliet (say) goodbye to Romeo, the Nurse (call).

Here are some examples from a modern love story:

i. Juliet (use) her computer when Romeo (phone) her.
j. While her parents (watch) TV, Juliet (leave) the house.
k. Romeo (not want) to meet Juliet because his favourite team (play) football.
l. Juliet (not answer) the phone because she (watch) a video.
m. While Tybalt and Benvolio (fight), the police (arrive).

ACTIVITIES

The Party

5 **Listen to Part Two of *Romeo and Juliet*.**
After the bells, you will hear a reporter describing the party at the house of the Capulets. In the text below, the letters (A) to (J) have replaced the NAMES of people or NUMBERS. Write the missing names and numbers here:

A ....   F ....
B ....   G ....
C ....   H ....
D ....   I ....
E ....   J ....

At the end of the report, you will hear a question. Copy it here:
How...?
What is the correct answer? You can check your answer on page 94.

Now listen again and complete the text below by filling gaps (1)-(21) with prepositions 'in', 'at', 'with' etc. Then listen and check your answers.

'I am standing [1].......... the big hall [2].......... the house of the Capulets. I am [3].......... the top [4].......... the stairs [5].......... the south entrance. [6].......... here, I can see the whole room.
A and **B** are standing [7].......... the centre [8].......... the room. They are watching **C** mysterious strangers [9].......... masks who have just come [10].......... the door. Perhaps they are Montagues. Is that why they are wearing masks? Will there be another fight?
D is standing [11].......... the bottom [12].......... the stairs. Her young beautiful daughter, **E**, is dancing [13].......... **F**. People say that they will get married one day. Juliet's **G** is [14].......... the couple. She is standing [15].......... the stairs and the dinner table. She is looking [16].......... the food and wine.
There are **H** other guests in the room and **I** servants. Also, there is a group [17].......... **J** musicians who are playing [18].......... a balcony [19].......... the dancers. It is a wonderful party. All the most important and famous people [20].......... Verona are here – [21].......... the Montagues!'

A C T I V I T I E S

Choosing

6 **Choosing the right person to marry.**

- Juliet chooses between Romeo and Paris.
- Romeo chooses between Rosaline and Juliet.

Juliet has a cousin, Mariana. She must choose between these two men who want to marry her:

JOHN:
I am poor but I want to marry you.
I am young and handsome.
I will be true to you.
I want you to be free.
We will live in a cottage.

RICHARD:
I am old but I am rich.
I want a young wife.
You must always do as I say.
You will have beautiful jewels and clothes.
You will live in a palace.

ACTIVITIES

When we are helping someone with a problem, we often say
'You should...'

For example:
Romeo should be careful.
Tybalt shouldn't fight so much.

Now use 'should', 'shouldn't' to write some advice for Mariana. Who should she marry? Why?

Romeo has a cousin, Benvolio. There are two women who love him. Write the things which they tell him. Which one should he marry? Why?

A Walk through Verona

Verona was born a very long time ago. In the year 100 A.D. it was already an important part of the Roman Empire. It became an important commercial, cultural and artistic centre because of its strategic location. It was located at the crossroads of three important Roman roads.

Verona was built according to the typical Roman city plan. The Forum was always the civic, political and religious centre of a Roman city. In the medieval days, when Romeo and Juliet lived in Verona, the Forum had become Piazza Erbe. Piazza Erbe was, and still is, the heart of the city centre.

The powerful Scaligeri family ruled Verona for more than a century, from 1259 to 1387. Cangrande I della Scala was responsible for the great cultural and artistic development of Verona. The symbol of the Scaligeri was a ladder, as in the surname 'della Scala'. This symbol is still visible on many monuments.

During the Renaissance, the important families of Verona decorated the outside walls of their splendid homes and palaces with enormous paintings, called frescos. These families loved their city and wanted to make it as beautiful as possible.

The Church of San Zeno, a splendid example of Romanesque architecture, was part of Romeo and Juliet's time. The huge Roman Amphitheatre, called the Arena, still remains in its original site. The medieval city grew around Piazza Erbe and the Arena.

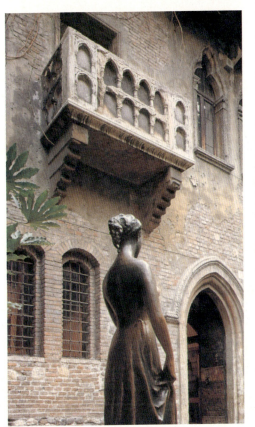

Romeo and Juliet lived in the medieval centre of the city, near the Adige River. Juliet's house was in Via Cappello, a very busy street of medieval Verona. Lots of hat-makers and wine cask-makers [1] had their shops there. The famous balcony, where she and Romeo met at night, is in the courtyard of her home.

Romeo's house was behind the Scaligeri tombs, not far from Juliet's house.

Another important part of medieval Verona was the beautiful convent of the Franciscan Friars, where Romeo and Juliet were secretly married. Juliet's tomb is in the crypt of the convent. Through the centuries, innumerable visitors such as Empress Maria Teresa of Austria, Charles Dickens and Lord Byron, have visited Juliet's tomb. People from all over the world, young and old, continue to visit Juliet's home, her tomb and her splendid city.

1. **wine cask-makers** : people who make wine casks.

Choose the correct answer:

1. Verona became an important commercial, cultural and artistic centre because
   - [ ] it was part of the Roman Empire
   - [ ] it won many wars
   - [ ] of its strategic location

2. According to the typical Roman city plan, the Forum was
   - [ ] an area for theatre and dance
   - [ ] the civic, political and religious centre
   - [ ] the main wall of the city

3. Piazza Erbe is
   - [ ] the heart of the city centre
   - [ ] the religious centre of Verona
   - [ ] where Romeo and Juliet met

4. Cangrande della Scala I, of the Scaligeri family,
   - [ ] was a bishop of the Church of San Zeno
   - [ ] was responsible for the great development of Verona
   - [ ] was a cruel Roman ruler

5. To make their city beautiful, the important families
   - [ ] decorated the outside walls of their homes and palaces
   - [ ] put the symbol of the ladder on their homes
   - [ ] put flowers and plants on their balconies

5. Juliet's house was
   - [ ] in Via delle arche Scaligere
   - [ ] near the Church of San Zeno
   - [ ] in Via Cappello

6. Romeo and Juliet were secretly married
   - [ ] in the Church of San Zeno
   - [ ] in the convent of the Franciscan Friars
   - [ ] in Piazza Erbe

PART THREE

The Prince of Cats

Romeo went to see Friar [1] Lawrence, his friend and teacher. The sun was rising [2] and it was a beautiful morning. The Friar was working in his garden. He was an expert gardener who knew all the plants – the poisonous [3] ones, the medicinal ones, the good and the bad ones.

'Friar,' said Romeo, 'I want to get married.'

'To Rosaline?' asked the Friar.

'No, I have forgotten Rosaline. She is nothing to me. I love Juliet and she loves me. You must help us. We want to get married today.'

1. **Friar** : a monk.
2. **rising** : coming up (to rise-rose-risen).
3. **poisonous** : it will kill you if you eat it.

PART THREE

'What? I see that young men's love is not in their hearts but in their eyes!'

'But Friar, you often told me that I was foolish to love Rosaline. Juliet is my true love.'

'Well, perhaps your marriage will make the Capulets and the Montagues friends. It is a good thing for Verona. I will help you.'

Benvolio and Mercutio were looking for Romeo in the streets of Verona.

'Poor Romeo,' said Benvolio. 'His heart is broken. Rosaline does not love him.'

'That's not his only problem,' replied Mercutio. 'Tybalt has challenged [1] him. He has sent a letter to his house. He wants to fight him.'

'But Tybalt is dangerous.'

'Yes. Tybalt is the Prince of Cats. He is an artist with his sword. [2] Romeo is a lamb. [3] He will die.'

'Here comes Romeo.'

'He is already dead. Rosaline has killed him with her cold eye! To him, she is more beautiful than Cleopatra. She is the most beautiful woman that ever lived. Lovers are fools!'

Mercutio called to Romeo. 'Where did you go last night after the party? You ran away from us.'

'Excuse me. I was busy.'

'Busy with Rosaline, eh? Forget love, Romeo. Remember your friends. Friendship is more important than love.'

'But look,' said Mercutio, 'here comes a fat old woman.'

1. **challenged** : invited to fight.
2. **an artist with his sword** : he fights very well.
3. **a lamb** : a young sheep, an innocent person.

Romeo and Juliet

It was the Nurse. Juliet had sent her to find Romeo. 'I must speak alone with you, sir,' she said.

Mercutio laughed. 'Is this your new girlfriend?' he asked.

'Go away,' said Romeo. 'Now, Nurse, what do you want?'

'First of all, I want you to promise that you will be kind to Juliet. She is very young. You must not hurt her.'

'I love her.'

'Then what do you want me to tell her?'

'Tell Juliet to come to Friar Lawrence's cell [1] this afternoon. We will get married there.'

'I love Juliet, sir. I remember when she was a little child. Look after her when you are her husband.'

The Nurse went back to Juliet who was waiting anxiously [2]. She told her the news. 'Tell your parents that you are going to pray,' [3] said the Nurse. 'Then go to see Friar Lawrence.'

The two lovers got ready [4] for their secret wedding.

In the afternoon, the sun was shining. Romeo went secretly to Friar Lawrence's cell.

'The day is bright,' said the Friar. 'It is a sign that the future will be happy.'

'I do not care [5] if I die tomorrow. It is enough that Juliet is mine.'

1. **cell** : the place where a friar lives.
2. **anxiously** : (G.) ängstlich, unruhig
3. **pray** : speak to God.
4. **got ready** : prepared themselves.
5. **I do not care** : it is not important to me.

PART THREE

'Don't be so passionate. It is better to love moderately. Then love will last [1] longer.'

At last Juliet arrived. She was very nervous. So was Romeo. They were very young but very much in love. Friar Lawrence was like a father to them. He took them into his cell and they were married.

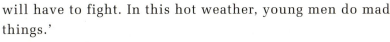

Meanwhile, Benvolio and Mercutio were walking in the streets of Verona. 'Let's go home,' said Benvolio. 'The Capulets are out in the streets. If we meet them, we will have to fight. In this hot weather, young men do mad things.'

'Don't worry. We are safe.'

'Here come the Capulets. Tybalt is there!'

'The Prince of Cats. I am not afraid.'

Tybalt approached Mercutio. 'I want to speak with you.'

'Do you want to speak or to fight?'

'You are not a Montague but a friend of Romeo. That makes you my enemy.'

'Be careful,' said Benvolio. 'We are in the public streets. If you fight, the Prince will be angry.'

At that moment, Romeo came back from his secret wedding.

'Fight, you villain!' [2] shouted Tybalt.

Romeo did not want to fight because Tybalt was Juliet's

---

1. **last** : endure, continue.
2. **villain** : (G.) Schurke.

Romeo and Juliet

cousin. 'I am not a villain. But I will not fight with you.'

Mercutio was angry because he thought that Romeo was a coward.¹ He took out his own sword.

'What do you want?' asked Tybalt.

'I want one of your nine lives, Prince of Cats!'

'I will fight you as Romeo is too afraid to fight,' agreed Tybalt.

Romeo came between Mercutio and Tybalt as they began to fight. 'Stop fighting. The Prince will be angry. He will punish you. Stop fighting! Stop, Tybalt! Stop, good Mercutio!' shouted Romeo.

But Tybalt took the opportunity to kill Mercutio. The sword passed under Romeo's arm as he stood between them. Then Tybalt ran quickly away.

Mercutio groaned.² 'Aaaaagh! I am hurt. I am dying. Romeo, this quarrel³ between your families has killed me.'

'Are you badly hurt?' asked Romeo.

'A scratch,⁴ a scratch. It's enough. Bring me a doctor.'

'Be brave, Mercutio. It cannot be so bad.'

'Look for me tomorrow in my grave.⁵ The Prince of Cats has killed me. Why did you come between us?'

'I wanted to help...'

Mercutio fell to the ground and died. It was Romeo's fault.⁶ His friend was dead.

1. **coward** : someone who is afraid.
2. **groaned** : cried with pain.
3. **quarrel** : argument, fight.
4. **scratch** : a small wound; a cat can scratch you.
5. **grave** : the place for a dead person under the ground.
6. **fault** : mistake, responsibility.

ACTIVITIES

Comprehension and Opinion

1 **What happened in Part Three?**

    a. Why did Friar Lawrence agree to help Romeo?
    b. Who was the Prince of Cats?
    c. What did Romeo tell the Nurse?
    d. What happened at Friar Lawrence's cell?
    e. Why did Romeo refuse to fight Tybalt?
    f. What was the result of the fight?

What do you think?

Mercutio said: 'Lovers are fools!' Do you agree?
Was Romeo responsible for his friend's death?

Animals and Character

2 Mercutio calls Tybalt 'the Prince of Cats' meaning that he is dangerous. He calls Romeo a 'lamb' meaning that he is gentle and innocent.
We often use animals when we are describing somebody figuratively.
Here are the names of some other creatures:

> dog   donkey   fox   horse   lion   mouse   owl   pig   swan

Fill in the gaps below with the most suitable word from the list. Use one animal name twice.

    a. He/She is as brave as a ....
    b.   "   as dirty as a ....
    c.   "   as strong as a ....
    d.   "   as timid as a ....

ACTIVITIES

e. He/She is as stupid as a ....
f. "   as clever as a   ....
g. "   as faithful as a ....
h. "   as wise as an   ....
i. "   as greedy as a   ....
j. "   as beautiful as a ....

The Present Perfect

3 **Do you remember these sentences?**

The Montagues and the Capulets have hated each other for hundreds of years.

Mercutio and Benvolio haven't seen Romeo since the party.

The verbs are in the Present Perfect Tense. We use this tense when we are talking about a period of time between the PAST and NOW. We often use it with 'for...' or 'since...'

For example:
He has lived in Rome for sixteen years.
She has lived in Vienna since 1994.

Here is an interview with some of the characters in the story. Write the complete questions and answers. Use 'for' or 'since' in the answers.

Interviewer: (How long/love/Juliet?)
How long have you loved Juliet?

Romeo: (I first saw her)
I've loved her since I first saw her.

ACTIVITIES

a. **Interviewer:** (How long/Romeo/be sad?)
....
Lady Capulet: (he fell in love withRosaline)
....

b. **Interviewer:** (How long/know/Romeo?)
....
Juliet: (twenty-four hours)
....

c. **Interviewer:** (How long/the Capulets/hate the Montagues?)
....
The Prince: (hundreds of years)
....

d. **Interviewer:** (How long/live/ Verona?)
....
The Friar: (fifty years)
....

e. **Interviewer:** (How long/look after Juliet?)
....
The Nurse: (she was a baby)
....

f. **Interviewer:** (How long/work for the Capulets?)
....
The Nurse: (I was fifteen years old)
....

What about you? What have you done since yesterday?
What have you done since the beginning of the year?
What have you never done in your life?
How long have you...?

For example:
I've had breakfast this morning.
I've been to five parties this year.
I've never driven a car.
I've known Theresa for seven years.

ACTIVITIES

The Nurse and Juliet

4 Listen to Part Three of *Romeo and Juliet* on the cassette.
After the bells, you will hear a conversation between Juliet and the Nurse. The Nurse has returned from the city where she has seen Romeo. Juliet wants to know the news but the Nurse makes her wait. Listen carefully. Complete Juliet's questions.

Juliet: Where ....?
Why ....? Ah, she's here.
Have ....?

Nurse: I am very tired. I have run from the town. My bones [1] ache. [2]

Juliet: What ....?

Nurse: Well, I have seen Romeo. He is handsome, young and polite. But have you had dinner yet?

Juliet: Nurse, don't ask stupid questions.
What ....?

Nurse: My head aches. I am very tired.

Juliet: I am sorry for you.
But sweet Nurse, what ....?

Nurse: He says... Where is your mother?

Juliet: She's in the house. But please be quick.
Is ....?

Nurse: Don't be angry. I have run all over the city for you. Next time, go and ask Romeo yourself.

Juliet: Sweet Nurse, please tell me.
Did ....?

Nurse: He wants to marry you at Friar Lawrence's cell this afternoon.

Juliet: Aaah! Thank you, Nurse.

1. **bones** : parts of the skeleton.
2. **ache** : hurt, cause pain.

ACTIVITIES

A Summary

5 Look at these pictures. They tell the story of Parts One, Two and Three of *Romeo and Juliet*.

1. fight

2. tell

3. decide

4. go

5. see

6. kiss

ACTIVITIES

7. jump

8. talk

9. meet

10. get married

11. fight

12. die

ACTIVITIES

What are the Past Simple forms of the verbs below the pictures?

1. fight   fought
2. tell   ....
3. decide   ....
4. go   ....
5. see   ....
6. kiss   ....
7. jump   ....
8. talk   ....
9. meet   ....
10. get   ....
11. fight   ....
12. die   ....

Now write your summary of the action. Put the verbs in the Past Tense and use the linking words to join some of them.
Begin:

The Montagues and the Capulets hated each other. One day they fought in the streets...

But then 2. .... Later, 3. .... 4. ....
At the party, ... 5. and 6. .... After the party,
7. .... 8. and, next day, 9. .... In the afternoon,
10. .... But in the city streets, 11. ....
12. ....

PART FOUR

Fortune's Fool[1]

At that moment, Tybalt returned.
'Boy!' shouted Tybalt. 'You came here with Mercutio and you will die as he did!'
Romeo was so angry that he lost control. He took out his sword and fought with Tybalt. He killed him.
'He killed my friend. Now he is dead. He is with Mercutio. Juliet, your love made me a coward but now I am brave.'
Benvolio took his arm. 'Romeo, you must escape. The people are coming. The Prince will punish you with death.'[2]
'Oh, I am Fortune's fool!' With those words, Romeo ran away.
Soon, the citizens arrived, followed by the Prince. They saw Mercutio and Tybalt lying dead on the ground.

---

1. **Fortune's Fool** : the victim of bad luck, of Fate.
2. **punish you with death** : Benvolio thinks the Prince will kill Romeo because he has killed Tybalt.

Romeo and Juliet

'Where are the people who began this fight?' asked the Prince angrily.

'I can tell you the complete story,' promised Benvolio.

'Oh Tybalt!' screamed [1] Lady Capulet. 'My brother's child. He has been murdered. A Montague must die for this.'

'Romeo wanted to stop the fight,' explained Benvolio. 'But Tybalt killed Mercutio. Then Romeo killed Tybalt.'

'He is lying!' [2] said Lady Capulet. 'He is a Montague. Romeo killed Tybalt. So Romeo must not live.'

'Romeo killed Tybalt. But Tybalt killed Mercutio,' said the Prince.

'Mercutio was Romeo's friend,' agreed Lord Montague. 'Romeo was right to kill his friend's killer.'

The Prince spoke seriously. 'No! It is wrong to kill. We banish [3] Romeo from Verona! If I find him in the city, he will die! We must not show mercy [4] to murderers.'

Those were the Prince's final words. Romeo had to leave Verona and never return.

Juliet was waiting for Romeo, her new husband. She wanted the night to come quickly so that they could be together. But when the Nurse arrived, she brought bad news.

'He is dead!'

'Who is dead?'

'I saw the body with my own eyes. He is dead.'

'What? Is Romeo dead?'

1. **screamed** : shouted in a high voice.
2. **lying** : not telling the truth.
3. **banish** : send away from the city, exile.
4. **mercy** : pity, forgiveness.

PART FOUR

'No, Tybalt is dead. Romeo has killed him. Romeo is banished, he must leave Verona.'

'Did Romeo kill my cousin? He is a villain. But I love him.'

Juliet was very unhappy. 'Your father and mother are crying for Tybalt,' the Nurse told her.

'I will cry for him too,' said Juliet. 'But I will cry longer for Romeo. I will never see him again. I will kill myself.'

'No,' said the Nurse. 'Romeo is hiding [1] with Friar Lawrence. I will bring him to you.'

'Yes, Nurse, bring him to me quickly. Give him this ring. He must come and say his last goodbye.'

Romeo was talking to Friar Lawrence. 'Everything is finished. I must leave Verona and never see Juliet again. Even a cat or a dog or a mouse may look at Juliet. But I cannot. Give me poison or a knife to kill myself.'

'You are mad. The Prince has shown mercy. He lets you live.'

'You are old, Friar. But I am young and in love. I want to die.'

'No, be brave. You must go to Mantua. You will be safe there. I will send you news about Juliet. One day, you will be together again. But here is the Nurse.'

'How is Juliet?' Romeo asked her immediately.

'She cries and cries. First, she calls out Tybalt's name, then she calls for Romeo. Then she falls on her bed.'

'Tonight, go with the Nurse,' said the Friar. 'See Juliet for the last time.'

---

1. **hiding** : staying in a secret place.

Romeo and Juliet

Romeo went back to the house of the Capulets. The Nurse took him into the garden. Nobody saw them.

'Here is a ladder,' [1] she said. 'Climb [2] up and go through the window.'

So Romeo spent his marriage night with Juliet.

Downstairs, in the house of the Capulets, Lord and Lady Capulet were talking. Lord Paris was with them.

'I will talk to Juliet. She will marry you next Wednesday...'

'That's too soon,' said Lady Capulet.

'On Thursday then. Tybalt is dead. There must be something good for the Capulet family – Juliet's wedding! I am her father. She will do as I say.'

Paris was very happy because he loved Juliet. Lord Capulet told his wife to see Juliet in the morning. She must prepare for her marriage. Her parents did not know that Juliet was already married to Romeo, the killer of her cousin Tybalt.

'I wish it was Thursday tomorrow,' said Paris.

'Well, goodbye until then,' said Lord Capulet. 'On Thursday, my daughter will marry you. I promise.'

1. **ladder** :
2. **climb** : go up.

PART FOUR

In the morning, Romeo left Juliet. He had to escape to Mantua before the Prince found him.

'Must you go?' asked Juliet. 'It is still night. The nightingale [1] is singing, not the lark.' [2]

'Look at the sky. The sun is rising. But I want to stay.'

'Go. It is dangerous for you here. But I want you to stay. Goodbye, sweet Romeo. Will I ever see you again?'

'Goodbye. I will think of you every second of the day.'

They kissed. Then Romeo climbed down the ladder.

'I can see only bad luck in the future,' said Juliet. 'I seem to see you dead.'

'Our sadness makes us think in this way. I will write every day. Goodbye.'

'Please, God, send him back to me again.'

1. **the nightingale** : a night bird.
2. **the lark** : a morning bird.

ACTIVITIES

Comprehension and Opinion

1 What happened in Part Four?

    a. Why did Romeo fight with Tybalt?
    b. What did the Prince decide?
    c. Did Juliet hate Romeo for killing Tybalt?
    d. Where did Romeo have to go?
    e. Why was Paris happy?
    f. Why was Juliet sad?

What do you think?

Was Romeo right to kill Tybalt? What should Juliet do?

Word Formation

2 Look at these words:

> lucky   luckier   luckiest   luckily   unluckily
> unlucky   unluckier   unluckiest   luck

All these words come from the word 'luck'. Put one suitable word from the list in each gap in the sentences below. You can use the same word more than once.

    a. Romeo and Juliet are the .... lovers in history.
    b. Mercutio had very bad ....
    c. ...., the Prince did not find Romeo.
    d. If Romeo has good ...., he will see Juliet again.
    e. Romeo is not very ....
    f. It was .... that Romeo and Juliet came from families which were enemies.

ACTIVITIES

g. During their fight, Tybalt was .... than Mercutio.
h. ...., Tybalt recognised Romeo at the party.
i. Before he left, Benvolio said, 'Good ....' to Romeo.
j. 'I will be the .... man in the world if you marry me,' said Romeo.

How many words can you make from:

| fortune   succeed   fail   die   friend   love   marry |

Already, Still and Yet

3 Look at these sentences about the story:

Juliet has *already* married Romeo
Romeo hasn't gone to Mantua *yet*.
Lord Capulet *still* wants Paris to marry Juliet.

Here are some short stories. Put *already* or *yet* or *still* in the gaps in the stories.

a. Susan expects to marry David. She has .... bought a wedding dress and invited a hundred guests. But David .... loves his old girlfriend, Julia. He hasn't forgotten her ....

b. It is .... January but Bill has .... sent a Valentine's card to his sweetheart, Rose. She hasn't sent him his Christmas present .... for last year. But he .... loves her.

c. Simon loves eating Italian food. This morning, he has .... eaten three dishes of pasta. He is .... hungry. 'Haven't you cooked dinner ....?' he asks his mother. 'No, I'm .... washing the dishes,' she answers.

d. Ben is going on holiday to Verona. He has .... been there six times. He loves the city because it is the city of Romeo and Juliet. 'Their ghosts haven't gone away ....,' he believes. 'They are .... talking together in the moonlit garden.'

ACTIVITIES

Four Zodiac Signs

4 Listen to Part Four of *Romeo and Juliet* on the cassette. After the bells, you will hear some horoscopes for next year about four signs of the Zodiac:

> Capricorn   Cancer   Leo   Libra

For each person, write GOOD or BAD or NORMAL on the appropriate line.

a. DEREK
    born: 8th January

    WORK ....
    LOVE ....
    SOCIAL LIFE ....
    TRAVEL ....
    HEALTH ....

b. REBECCA
    born: 23rd October

    WORK ....
    LOVE ....
    SOCIAL LIFE ....
    TRAVEL ....
    HEALTH ....

c. ROBERT
    born: 18th August

    WORK ....
    LOVE ....
    SOCIAL LIFE ....
    TRAVEL ....
    HEALTH ....

d. SARAH
    born: 11th July

    WORK ....
    LOVE ....
    SOCIAL LIFE ....
    TRAVEL ....
    HEALTH ....

ACTIVITIES

Horoscopes

5 What do you think will happen to Derek, Rebecca, Robert and Sarah next year? Use the information from Activity 4 to predict their futures. Remember to use the future form of the verbs with 'will'.

For example:
Derek will find a very good job next year. It will pay him a big salary. He will meet a beautiful actress and they will get married. After they are married, they will go to lots of parties together. They will travel to the Bahamas, to the USA and to India. He will not be ill at any time. Lucky Derek!

A Bad Luck Story

6 Are you lucky or unlucky?
Write down three lucky things that have happened to you.

For example:
My favourite football team always wins.

Write down three unlucky things that have happened to you.
For example:
I was ill on my birthday.

Then write down three things that people think are lucky.
For example:
Seeing a black cat is lucky.

Then write down three things that are unlucky.
For example:
Breaking a mirror is unlucky.

ACTIVITIES

Now write a story about an unlucky person.

For example, you can write about:
someone who had a winning lottery ticket but lost it...
someone who wanted to play football for his country but broke his leg...
someone who failed an important examination because he/she was ill...

Call your story: 'FORTUNE'S FOOL.'

Life in Renaissance Verona

During the Renaissance, social class and dress were closely related. Rich families had beautiful clothes made for them. Silk, satin, brocade, gold, and precious jewels were used for the clothes of important men, women and children.

Wealthy men and boys wore coloured leggings [1] and elaborate shirts, jackets and mantels. They also wore hats with coloured feathers. Often, the colours of the clothes were those of the family coat of arms. [2]

1. leggings :
2. coat of arms :

Young girls and women of rich families wore dresses that were very ornamental. These dresses were decorated with precious stones, pearls, gold and silver threads. It usually took many years to make a dress! Several servants and tailors worked on only one dress. The poor dressed with simple clothes of wool or cotton, with no decoration.

Young boys and men wore a dagger [1] on their belt for protection. Some also carried a sword. Family feuds [2] were common in those days, and there were often street fights.

A horse was a status symbol. Only the members of important families rode a horse. The others went on foot.

The upper classes often gave costume balls in the dance halls of their enormous homes and palaces. Only those who were invited could go to the ball.

1. **dagger** :
2. **feuds** : hatred or violence which continue over a long period of time, between people or families.

Things have certainly changed in our times. Men and women, rich and poor, usually dress in a similar way.

Many clothes are unisex! We don't have our clothes made by hand. We buy them in shops.

Today we don't carry daggers or swords. Most young people have a means of transportation—either a bicycle, a scooter, a motorbike or a car. We don't need a special invitation to go dancing. We simply go to a disco, whenever we want.

However, one habit has remained the same: the late afternoon walk in the main road or square. Just as Romeo and his friends met in the main square of Verona, our young people do the same. They meet, take a walk and talk in the main road or square of their city or town.

Word Puzzle

Find the word in the text to match these descriptions:

1. a soft, shiny cloth : _ _ _ _ _
2. a precious stone : _ _ _ _ _ _
3. a person who makes clothes : _ _ _ _ _ _ _
4. a type of knife : _ _ _ _ _ _ _
5. a big, formal dance : _ _ _ _ _
6. an old means of transportation : _ _ _ _ _ _
7. clothes that both men and women wear : _ _ _ _ _ _ _

PART FIVE

My Lady's Dead!

Early next morning, Lady Capulet visited Juliet in her bedroom. 'Daughter, are you awake?'

'It is very early. I am not well,' answered Juliet.

'Are you still crying for your cousin Tybalt? It is good to cry. But now it is time to stop.'

'Let me cry more for my poor cousin.'

'Well, really you should cry because Romeo, his killer, is still alive.'

'Yes, mother. I wish I could see Romeo now and... kill him.'

'I will send a servant to Mantua to poison him,' promised Lady Capulet. 'He will not live long. But Juliet, I have good news for you. You will get married to Paris early next Thursday morning. Then you will be happy.'

'No, mother. It is impossible. I don't want to get married so soon. Tell my father this. As you know, I hate Romeo. He has

PART FIVE

killed my cousin. But I'd rather [1] marry Romeo than Paris.'

'Here comes your father. Tell him yourself.'

'What?' said Lord Capulet. 'Are you still crying? Wife, have you told her the news?'

'Yes. The little fool thanks you but she won't marry Paris.'

Lord Capulet was very angry.
'Lord Paris is a very fine gentleman. This is a great opportunity.'

'Thank you, father, but I will not marry him.'

'Are you too proud [2] to marry him? Put on a wedding dress next Thursday and go with Paris to the church. If you don't, I'll pull you there by the hair.'

'Good father, listen to me.'

'Don't argue [3] with me. Go to the church next Thursday. I'm glad we have no more children like this.'

'Please don't be angry with my little Juliet, sir,' said the Nurse.

'Shut up, you fat old fool!'

'Be calm,' Lady Capulet told him.

'I have decided. If you don't obey me, [4] I will throw you out in the street.'

1. **I'd rather** : I would prefer.
2. **are you too proud** : (here) do you think you are too superior?
3. **argue** : disagree.
4. **obey me** : follow my instructions, do as I say.

Romeo and Juliet

When her parents had gone, Juliet asked the Nurse for advice.[1]
'I already have a husband that I love. What should I do?'
'Well, Romeo is not here. Paris is a fine gentleman, it's true. He is more handsome than Romeo. Forget Romeo and marry Paris.'
'Do you speak from your heart?'
'Of course,' said the Nurse.
Juliet realised that she could not trust[2] the Nurse. She went to Friar Lawrence to ask his advice.
The Friar was very worried. Paris was talking to him and had told him that he would marry Juliet.
'Does she love you?' asked the Friar.
'I don't know. We haven't talked about love because she is weeping[3] for her cousin's death. But our marriage will make her happy again.'
'But look, here comes Juliet.'
'Welcome, my lady and my wife,' said Paris. 'Have you come to tell the Friar that you love me?'
'I cannot answer that,' said Juliet. 'But please, let me talk to the Friar privately.'
When they were alone, the Friar told Juliet to be happy. 'If you are brave[4] enough, I have a plan that will help you and Romeo. You will be together again.'
'What must I do? I will do anything for Romeo, my husband.'
'Go home and agree to marry Paris.'
'No! I cannot.'

1. **advice** : help, guidance.
2. **trust** : believe in, be friendly with.
3. **weeping** : crying.
4. **brave** : courageous.

PART FIVE

'Listen carefully. On Wednesday night, go to your bedroom alone. Take this bottle and drink the liquid. It is a special potion.¹ You will sleep for forty-two hours. Your family will think that you are dead. They will carry you to the tomb² of the Capulets. Meanwhile, I will send a message to Romeo. He will come secretly to the tomb. When you wake up, you can escape together. Are you brave enough to do this, Juliet?'

'Give me the bottle, Friar. Love will give me strength.'

Juliet went home. Lord and Lady Capulet were very happy when she told them that she had met Paris at Friar Lawrence's cell and that she would marry him.

'Now I am going to my room to pray. Do not come with me, Nurse, I want to be alone.'

In her room, Juliet looked at the bottle of mysterious liquid which Friar Lawrence had given her.

'I am afraid. Perhaps it is poison. Or perhaps I will wake in the tomb and Romeo will not be there. I will be alone in the middle of all the dead bodies with my dead cousin, Tybalt. It will be terrible.'

Bravely, Juliet picked up the bottle and raised it to her lips. 'Romeo, Romeo, I drink to you!'

She drank. She fell on the bed and slept.

The next morning, it was Thursday. The Nurse came to wake her up for her marriage. 'You lazy girl,' she said. 'You mustn't lie

1. **potion** : a drink with a special effect.
2. **tomb** : a place to put dead people.

Romeo and Juliet

in bed on your wedding day... Help! Help! My lady's dead!'
95   Lord and Lady Capulet ran to their daughter's room.
'She's dead, she's dead, she's dead,' cried Lady Capulet.
'Her body is cold. I cannot speak,' said Lord Capulet.
At that moment, Paris and Friar Lawrence entered the house. 'Is Juliet ready to go to the church?' asked the Friar.
100   'Oh Paris,' said Lord Capulet, 'death has taken your wife.'
The Nurse began to cry. 'O terrible day! O sad day! O horrible day! There has never been such a black day. O sad day! O unhappy day!'
'Do not be sad,' said the Friar. 'Juliet is in
105   Heaven. She is happier there than when she was alive.'
'The wedding must become a funeral,' said Lord Capulet. 'Tell the musicians to play sad tunes.¹ Put the wedding flowers
110   on my daughter's body.'
Lord and Lady Capulet took Juliet to the tomb of the Capulets. The Nurse, Lord Paris and Friar Lawrence followed her body. The Friar was the only one who knew
115   the secret – Juliet was alive. He was thinking: 'I have sent Friar John to Mantua to tell Romeo to come back to Verona. He will be here when Juliet wakes up.'

1. **tunes** : music.

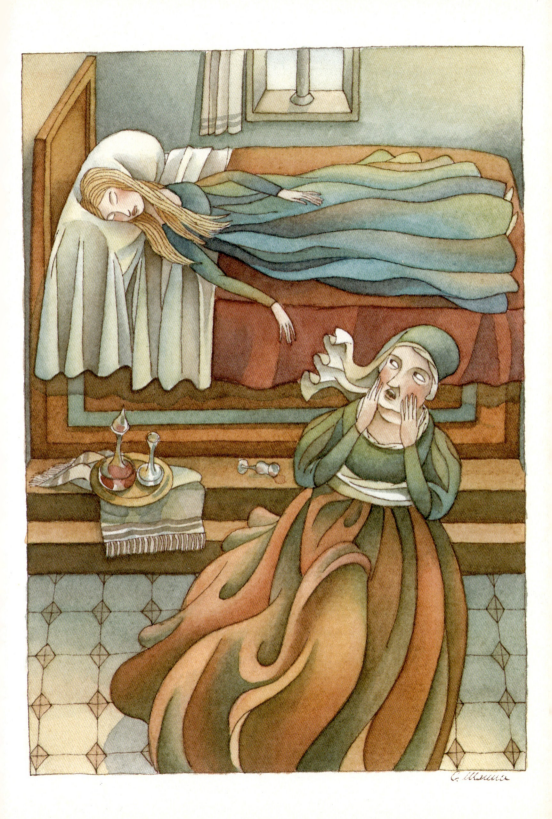

ACTIVITIES

Comprehension and Opinion

1 **What happened in Part Five?**

    a. What did Lady Capulet tell Juliet?
    b. What did Lord Capulet say he would do to Juliet?
    c. What did the Nurse tell Juliet to do?
    d. How long would Juliet sleep after drinking the liquid?
    e. What did Juliet say as she drank the liquid?
    f. Why had Friar John gone to Mantua?

What do you think?

Will the Friar's plan succeed? What will happen if Friar John doesn't reach Mantua in time?

Ought to

2 **Lord Capulet says:** 'You ought to be grateful.'

We use 'ought to': to give advice
For example:
You ought to learn Spanish.

to remind somebody of their duty (= their responsibilities.)
For example:
You ought to pay taxes.

Using 'ought to', write down three things:

    a. that parents say to children.
        for example: 'You ought to go to bed.'

    b. that teachers say to pupils.
        for example: 'You ought not to be late.'

ACTIVITIES

c. that viewers say about television.
   for example: 'They ought to show more films.'

d. that a director says to an actress.
   for example: 'You ought to speak more loudly.'

e. that a referee says to a footballer.

f. that a teenager says to his/her parents.

g. that a driver says about another driver.

h. that a wife says to her husband or a husband to his wife.

Parents and Children

3 Juliet's parents wanted to make her marry Paris. What should parents decide for their children? Fill in the table below to show what you think. Put a cross (X) for 'NO' and a tick (✔) for 'YES'.

PARENTS SHOULD DECIDE:

age of child in years	9-10	11-12	13-14	15-16
a. The time they come home at night:	☐	☐	☐	☐
b. The TV programmes they watch:	☐	☐	☐	☐
c. The time they go to bed:	☐	☐	☐	☐
d. The time they spend on homework:	☐	☐	☐	☐
e. Where they go on holiday:	☐	☐	☐	☐
f. The kind of clothes they wear:	☐	☐	☐	☐
g. The friends they go out with:	☐	☐	☐	☐

Discuss your answers with your classmates.

Then write a dialogue between a child and his/her parents. They cannot agree about some of the things in the table.

For example, here is the beginning of a conversation:

ACTIVITIES

JOHN: Goodbye Dad, goodbye Mum.
FATHER: Where are you going?
MOTHER: What time are you coming back?
JOHN: Don't ask so many questions.
FATHER: Don't be so cheeky. We're your parents.
MOTHER: It's not safe in the streets late at night. You must be back by half-past eight...

Past Perfect versus Past Simple

4 Look at this sentence:

> After Romeo had met the servant, he went to the party. **There are two actions in the PAST – 'had met' and 'went'. We use the Past Perfect form for the earlier action:** *had met* **and the Past Simple for the later action:** *went*

In each sentence below, put one of the verbs in the Past Perfect and one in the Past Simple:

a. Romeo (be) in love with Rosaline before he (see) Juliet.
b. After he (hear) her speaking on her balcony, he (know) that she loved him.
c. Tybalt (challenge) Romeo to fight because he (go) to the Capulets' party.
d. After Tybalt (kill) Mercutio, Romeo (lose) control.
e. The Prince (send) Romeo away because he (kill) Tybalt.
f. Paris (not know) that Juliet (marry) Romeo.
g. Although the Nurse (help) Romeo, later she (tell) Juliet to marry Paris.
h. Juliet (drink) from the bottle that the Friar (give) her.
i. After she (drink) the liquid, she (fall) asleep.
j. The Nurse (think) that Juliet was asleep but then she (think) that she was dead.

ACTIVITIES

Now use these verbs to make similar sentences. Use each Past Perfect verb with any Past Simple verb.

| had written | had seen | had driven | had arrived |
| had eaten | had taken | had found | had finished |

For example:

After Shakespeare had written 'Romeo and Juliet', he began to write his next play.

a. ....

b. ....

c. ....

d. ....

e. ....

f. ....

g. ....

h. ....

ACTIVITIES

True and false

5 **Listen to Part Five of *Romeo and Juliet*.**
After the bells, you will hear twelve statements about the story repeated twice. ELEVEN of them are not completely true. For each one, write down the truth.

For example, if you hear:
Romeo was Mercutio's brother.
write:
Romeo was Mercutio's **friend**.
Be careful! ONE of the statements is true.

1. ....
2. ....
3. ....
4. ....
5. ....
6. ....
7. ....
8. ....
9. ....
10. ....
11. ....
12. ....

ACTIVITIES

The Verona Times

6 Answer these questions about the end of Part Five.
   a. What is the name of the dead person?
   b. How old was she?
   c. Who are her parents?
   d. Who found her?
   e. What time was it?
   f. How did she die?
   g. What special day was it?
   h. Who was going to marry her?
   i. How did her parents feel?
   j. Where did they take her?

Now use this information to write the front page of *the Verona Times*.

THE VERONA TIMES

MYSTERY DEATH OF ONLY DAUGHTER

Write another front page for *the Verona Times*.
Write the news on the day that Mercutio and Tybalt died.

PART SIX

With a Kiss, I Die

Romeo was in the city of Mantua.
'I have been dreaming about Juliet. I was dead but when she kissed me I became a king. Even a dream of love is sweet. This dream has made me happy.'
At that moment, his servant Balthasar, found him. He had come with the latest news from Verona.
'Balthasar! What is the news from Verona? Have you got letters from the Friar? How is my mother? How is my father? How is Juliet?'
His servant replied sadly. 'Juliet is dead. She lies in the tomb of the Capulets.'
'What! Get me some horses. I will ride to Verona tonight.'
When Balthasar had gone, Romeo made his plans. 'I will go to the tomb. I will kiss her for the last time. Then I will drink poison. If Juliet is dead, I will die too.' He began to think

PART SIX

carefully. 'There is an apothecary ¹ who has a shop near here. He is very poor. If I pay him well, he will sell me some poison.'

So Romeo went to the apothecary and gave him some gold.

'Here is the poison. It is enough to kill twenty men.'

In the middle of the night, Paris was at the tomb of the Capulets. He had come to put flowers on Juliet's grave.

'Sweet Juliet,' said Paris, 'I will visit your grave every night and cry for you. But someone is coming. I will hide and watch...'

Romeo arrived at the tomb with his servant. 'Give this letter to my father tomorrow morning, Balthasar. Now go away. Don't try to stop me. I am stronger than tigers or the roaring ² sea.'

Romeo used a strong metal bar to open the tomb. Paris was watching. 'This is Romeo, who murdered Juliet's cousin. He has come here to damage the tomb. I will arrest him!'

Paris called to Romeo. 'You are a Montague, the one who killed Tybalt. You must die!'

'I do not know you,' said Romeo. 'Go away if you want to live. Do not fight with me. I am desperate.' ³

'I arrest you, murderer!' said Paris.

1. **apothecary** : a pharmacist, a person who sells medicines etc.
2. **roaring** : making a great sound, like a lion or tiger.
3. **desperate** : (G.) verzweifelt.

Romeo and Juliet

They began to fight.

Romeo fought like a madman. He was stronger than Paris and killed him.

'Put my body with Juliet,' cried Paris as he died.

Romeo knelt down [1] to look at his face.

'It is Paris! Balthasar told me that he wanted to marry Juliet. We are both unlucky. But where is Juliet? I must look at her beauty for the last time.'

Romeo went inside the tomb. He saw Juliet lying there and thought that she was dead.

'Oh my love, my wife! Death has kissed you. But you are still beautiful. Death is jealous. [2] He keeps you here as his lover. I will also stay here. But let me hold you in my arms. I love you.'

Romeo held Juliet. He took a cup of poison out of his pocket and raised it to his lips.

Outside, someone was calling him: 'Romeo! Romeo!'

He kissed Juliet. 'With a kiss, I die.'

Meanwhile, Friar John had come to Friar Lawrence's cell.

'Have you given my letter to Romeo, Friar John?'

'No, Friar Lawrence. I did not reach [3] Mantua. There was plague [4] in one of the villages on the road and the soldiers did not let me pass.'

'What! This is bad news. If Juliet wakes when Romeo is not there, she will be afraid. I must go to her.'

1. **knelt down** : went down on his knees.
2. **jealous** : (G.) eifersüchtig, neidisch.
3. **reach** : arrive at.
4. **plague** : a very serious illness that spreads quickly.

PART SIX

Friar Lawrence hurried¹ to the tomb. He met Balthasar.

'I can see a light in the tomb. Who is looking among the skulls² and the worms?'³

'It is my master, Romeo.'

'How long has he been there?'

'Half an hour. I was sleeping but I dreamt there was a fight between my master and another man.'

'I must go to him. Romeo! Romeo!'

But when the Friar went inside the tomb, Romeo had already drunk the poison. He was dead.

Inside the tomb, it was cold and dark. Juliet woke up and saw the Friar.

'Where is Romeo?' she asked.

'He is dead,' replied the Friar. 'Paris is also dead. But we must go. The Watchman⁴ is coming. Come with me. I will take you to the nuns⁵ who will let you live with them.'

'No, I will stay with Romeo,' said Juliet.

The Friar left her. Juliet held Romeo in her arms.

'I will drink poison too – but the cup is empty. Let me kiss his lips. They are still warm. But I can hear people coming.'

Outside the tomb, the Watchman was approaching.

'Quick, here is Romeo's dagger. Let me die!'

Juliet stabbed⁶ herself and fell.

1. **hurried** : went quickly.
2. **skull** : hard bone of the head.
3. **worms** : small animals with a long, thin body, no bones and no legs.
4. **Watchman** : a kind of policeman.
5. **nuns** : religious women who live without men.
6. **stabbed** : killed with a knife.

Romeo and Juliet

Everyone arrived at the tomb of the Capulets. It was too late. Romeo and Juliet had both died. Their great love story was finished.

'Here is the body of Paris,' said the Watchman. 'And here are the bodies of a boy and girl.'

'Juliet!' cried Lord Capulet. 'There is blood and a dagger. Our only daughter is dead. This is a terrible day for the Capulets.'

Lord Montague spoke: 'Last night, my wife died from a broken heart because Romeo was banished from Verona. Now *he* is dead, poisoned. This is a terrible day for the Montagues.'

'I can explain everything,' said the Friar. 'It is all a mistake, a terrible mistake. They loved each other. The Nurse and I helped them to get married secretly. Now they are dead.'

Finally the Prince spoke.

'My friends Mercutio and Paris are dead. Tybalt is dead. Romeo and Juliet are dead. This is a terrible day for Verona. Lord Montague and Lord Capulet, shake hands. Your families must be friends. Love will change the world!'

A C T I V I T I E S

Comprehension and Opinion

1 **What happened in Part Six?**

    a. What did Romeo decide to do?
    b. Why did Paris and Romeo fight?
    c. Was Juliet really dead when Romeo saw her?
    d. Why did Friar Lawrence's plan not succeed?
    e. How did Juliet kill herself?
    f. What did the Prince say?

What do you think?

Who is responsible for the deaths? Will the Montagues and the Capulets be friends?

Past Simple Passive

2 We can write:
Romeo killed Paris. (Past Simple Active)
or *Paris was killed by Romeo.* (Past Simple Passive).
Change these sentences in the same way from Active to Passive. Use 'was' or 'were' + the past participle.

    a. Tybalt killed Mercutio and then Romeo killed Tybalt.
    b. The Prince banished Romeo.
    c. The Friar hid Romeo in his cell. Luckily, the Prince did not find him.
    d. Juliet sent the Nurse to find Romeo. She took him to the garden of the Capulets at night.
    e. The Capulets put Juliet's body in the tomb.
    f. The soldiers prevented Friar John from reaching Mantua.
    g. The Watchman found three dead bodies.
    h. The Friar helped Romeo and Juliet.
    i. Shakespeare wrote *Romeo and Juliet* and the actors* performed it in London. (*'by the actors' is not important, so forget it.)

ACTIVITIES

The Verona Times

3 What happened in Parts Four, Five and Six of the story? Answer these questions to help you to remember.

- a. What happened after Mercutio was killed?
- b. What did the Prince do?
- c. Where did Romeo hide?
- d. What was arranged by Lord and Lady Capulet?
- e. What did Juliet do, with the Friar's help?
- f. Where did the Capulets take Juliet? Why?
- g. Why did Romeo come back to Verona?
- h. Who did he meet at the tomb? What happened?
- i. What did Romeo see and do in the tomb?
- j. What did Juliet do after she had woken up?
- k. What did the Watchman find?
- l. What did the Capulets and the Montagues decide to do?

Now write a front page story for the Verona Times.
Arrange the information in the best order.
Think carefully about the tenses of the verbs that you use.

THE VERONA TIMES

TRAGIC DEATH OF YOUNG LOVERS
Friar tells everything

Lines from Shakespeare

4 After the bells, you will hear some famous lines from Shakespeare's original play. Remember that Shakespeare wrote 400 years ago, so the language is old-fashioned and difficult! Which character is speaking? Can you decide at which moment in the story the lines are from?

a. Thou * wast the prettiest babe that e'r I nursed.
An I might live to see thee * married once, I have my wish.
* **Thou, thee, thy**: old forms of 'you, you and your'.

b. For you and I are past our dancing days.

c. It seems she hangs upon the cheek * of night
As a rich jewel in an Ethiope's ear.
* **cheek**: the side of the face.

d. My only love sprung* from my only hate!
* **sprung**: (past participle of 'to spring') come from.

e. But soft, what light through yonder * window breaks?
It is the east, and Juliet is the sun.
* **yonder**: that.

f. See how she leans her cheek upon her hand.
O, that I were a glove upon that hand,
That I might touch that cheek!

g. O Romeo, Romeo, wherefore art thou * Romeo?
Deny thy father and refuse thy name,
* **Wherefore art thou**: Why are you called…

h. What's in a name? That which we call a rose
By any other word would smell as sweet.

i. O, swear * not by the moon, th'inconstant moon *
* **swear**: promise seriously.
* **th'inconstant moon**: the changeable moon.

j. Good night, good night. Parting is such sweet sorrow
That I shall say good night till it be morrow.

k. Young men's love then lies
Not truly in their hearts, but in their eyes.

l. A plague o' both your houses *.
They have made worms' meat of me.
* **houses**: here, families.

m. For never was a story of more woe *
Than this of Juliet and her Romeo.
* **woe**: sadness.

A C T I V I T I E S

Characters in the Play

5 Here are some opinions about the story. In each box, write:
   A if you agree.
   D if you disagree.
   ? if you are not sure.

   a. Romeo and Juliet were too young to love.
   b. Lord Capulet was a bad father.
   c. The Prince was not strict (= strong) enough.
   d. Lord Montague and Capulet were responsible for the lovers' deaths.
   e. Romeo was a murderer.
   f. Juliet was right to kill herself.
   g. Friar Lawrence made a lot of mistakes.
   h. Tybalt was the cause of all the problems.
   i. Benvolio was the best person in the story.
   j. The Nurse was a foolish old woman.

Compare your answers with your partner's.

ACTIVITIES

All the Romeos and all the Juliets

6 Here is a short poem:

> *The Capulets hated the Montagues*
> *who hated the Capulets;*
> *there were angry words in Verona*
> *and blood running in the streets.*
> *But after the death of a boy and girl,*
> *their love lived on to change the world,*
> *and so does the love of all the Romeos and all the Juliets.*

Today, there are modern Romeos and Juliets.
Maybe they come:
  from different social classes
  or from opposite sides in a war
  or from different races
  or from different gangs
  or from the supporters of different football teams
  or from different galaxies!

Think of ideas for a story about one of these.
Maybe your 'Romeo and Juliet' will be as famous as Shakespeare's.

Answer to exercise 5, page 39.
There are 59 people in the room. Did you include the reporter?

Juliet through the Centuries

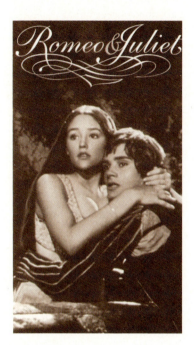

Juliet Capulet is undoubtedly one of the best known characters of literature. She lived long ago, and yet people all over the world know her tragic love story. She and Romeo are considered the eternal symbol of love, everywhere.

There have been countless love stories, happy ones and sad ones. And yet, this tragic love story has been remembered and retold through the centuries, in many different ways.

Poets have written poems about the two young lovers. The great Italian poet, Dante Alighieri, mentions the two feuding families in his *Divina Commedia* (Purgatorio). Artists have created paintings on this subject. Musicians have written music for operas, symphonies and ballets, all based on Shakespeare's play. These are a few examples:

Vincenzo Bellini	Capuleti e Montecchi	(opera)	1830
Hector Berlioz	Giulietta e Romeo	(symphony)	1839
Charles Gounod	Romeo and Juliet	(opera)	1867
Peter I. Tchaikovsky	Romeo and Juliet	(tone poem)	1892
Sergei Prokofiev	Romeo and Juliet	(ballet)	1936

There have been numerous film productions, too. In 1968, Franco Zeffirelli directed the excellent film, *Romeo e Giulietta.* Another very recent film version is *Romeo and Juliet,* with Leonard Di Caprio.

The famous American musical *West Side Story* is a modern version of the eternal love story. *West Side Story* takes place in the immigrant neighbourhoods of New York City

in the 1950's. Instead of two enemy families, there are two young enemy gangs. The famous American orchestra conductor and composer, Leonard Bernstein, wrote the exciting music for this wonderful musical.

Juliet has been represented and interpreted in many different ways through the years. The Juliet we see in *West Side Story,* for example, represents the typical young girl of the twentieth century. She is very different from Shakespeare's heroine. Her appearance, her language, her aspirations and her life are very different. But the sentiments of love and passion remain the same through the centuries.

Are the following sentences true or false? Correct the false ones.

	T	F
1. Juliet and Romeo are considered the eternal symbol of love, all over the world	☐	☐
2. Dante Alighieri mentions the two lovers in his *Divina Commedia*.	☐	☐
3. The Italian composer, Vincenzo Bellini, wrote a song about Juliet.	☐	☐
4. The Russian composer Prokofiev wrote a ballet called *Romeo and Juliet*.	☐	☐
5. Leonard Bernstein, the contemporary American composer, wrote a tone poem called *West Side Story*.	☐	☐
6. *West Side Story* takes place in New York City in the 1950's.	☐	☐
7. Instead of two feuding families, there are two enemy gangs.	☐	☐

Romeo and Juliet

PLAYSCRIPT

ACT ONE

THE MONTAGUES AND THE CAPULETS

In the beautiful city of Verona, there are two families – the Montagues and the Capulets. They hate each other. They have hated each other for hundreds of years. One day, the servants begin to fight in the streets.

SERVANTS OF THE MONTAGUES : The Montagues are better than the Capulets!

SERVANTS OF THE CAPULETS : Our masters, the Capulets, are better!

Then Benvolio and Tybalt arrive.

BENVOLIO : Stop fighting!

TYBALT : Fight with me, Benvolio.

BENVOLIO : No! Fighting is stupid!

TYBALT : Your sword is out. Fight!

Then Lord and Lady Capulet arrive. Lord Capulet is old but he wants to fight too.

LORD CAPULET : Bring me my sword.

LADY CAPULET : You are too old to fight. You don't need a sword, you need a crutch.

Then Lord and Lady Montague arrive. Soon everyone is fighting. It is very dangerous. At last, the Prince arrives. He is very angry.

PRINCE : Stop fighting! I want peace in my city. Lord Capulet and Lord Montague, you are old but you are not wise. If your two families fight again, you will both die!

LORD CAPULET : I, Lord Capulet, promise not to fight again.

LORD MONTAGUE : I, Lord Montague, promise not to fight again.

The Prince is happy. Everyone goes away.

PAUSE

Lady Montague and Benvolio are talking.

BENVOLIO : Tybalt wants to kill all the Montagues. He is very dangerous.

LADY MONTAGUE : Where is my son, Romeo? Is he safe?

BENVOLIO : He is not here. He is walking by himself in the forest. He is sad.

LADY MONTAGUE : Why is he sad?

BENVOLIO : I don't know. But look, he is coming now. I will ask him.
Why are you unhappy, Romeo?

ROMEO : I am in love.

BENVOLIO : Who do you love?

ROMEO : I love sweet Rosaline. She is beautiful, intelligent and good. But she does not love me. That is why I am sad.

BENVOLIO : Forget her. There are many other girls.

ROMEO : No, I can never forget her.

PAUSE

Lord Capulet is talking to his wife, Lady Capulet.

LORD CAPULET : I am going to have a party. I will invite all the important people from Verona. But not the Montagues.

LADY CAPULET : You must invite Paris.

LORD CAPULET : Yes, I want him to meet Juliet. One day, they will get married.

LADY CAPULET : I like that idea. I will go and tell Juliet.

LORD CAPULET : Tell my servant to come here.

SERVANT : Yes, my Lord?

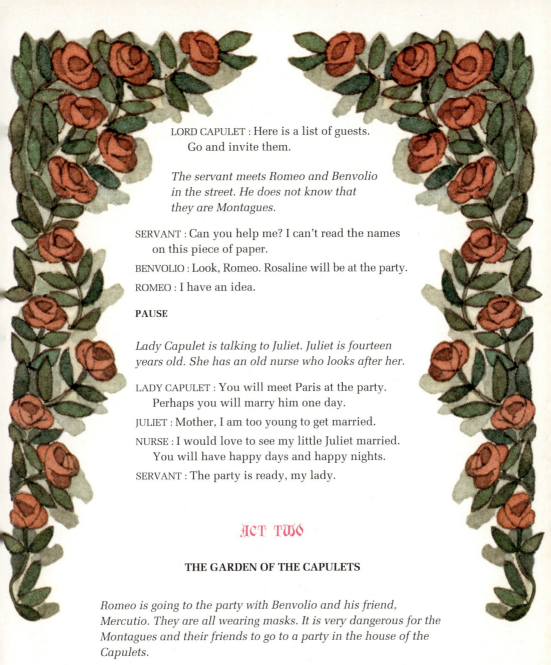

LORD CAPULET : Here is a list of guests.
 Go and invite them.

The servant meets Romeo and Benvolio in the street. He does not know that they are Montagues.

SERVANT : Can you help me? I can't read the names on this piece of paper.
BENVOLIO : Look, Romeo. Rosaline will be at the party.
ROMEO : I have an idea.

PAUSE

Lady Capulet is talking to Juliet. Juliet is fourteen years old. She has an old nurse who looks after her.

LADY CAPULET : You will meet Paris at the party. Perhaps you will marry him one day.
JULIET : Mother, I am too young to get married.
NURSE : I would love to see my little Juliet married. You will have happy days and happy nights.
SERVANT : The party is ready, my lady.

ACT TWO

THE GARDEN OF THE CAPULETS

Romeo is going to the party with Benvolio and his friend, Mercutio. They are all wearing masks. It is very dangerous for the Montagues and their friends to go to a party in the house of the Capulets.

ROMEO : Put on your masks. They must not recognise us. I cannot wait to see fair Rosaline.
SERVANT : Welcome, gentlemen. Come in. Dance and drink and eat. Enjoy yourselves.

*As they go into the house, Romeo sees Juliet for the first time.
He forgets Rosaline! He falls in love! But Tybalt recognises Romeo's voice.*

ROMEO : Who is that lady? She is more beautiful than the moon. I have never loved until now.

TYBALT : I know his voice. It is a Montague. I will kill him.

LORD CAPULET : Be calm, Tybalt. This is a party. I want no trouble.

Romeo goes to Juliet and talks to her. He does not know who she is.

ROMEO : My lips are ready to kiss you.

JULIET : But I do not know you.

ROMEO : I must kiss you.

JULIET : Here I am. My lips are here.

Romeo kisses Juliet. He kisses her a second time.

NURSE : Juliet, your mother wants you. You must come with me.

ROMEO : Excuse me, who is that girl?

NURSE : Young man, that is Juliet. She is a Capulet.

ROMEO : *(thinking aloud)* What! I am in love with the daughter of the enemy of my family.

JULIET : Nurse, who is that young man?

NURSE : That is Romeo. He is a Montague.

JULIET : Oh no! I am in love with the son of the enemy of my family. We can never get married.

After they leave the party, Mercutio and Benvolio look for Romeo.

MERCUTIO : Look! He is there in the shadows. What is he doing?

BENVOLIO : He is jumping the wall. He is going into the garden of the Capulets.

MERCUTIO : Romeo! Madman! Lover! He is going to look for Rosaline.

BENVOLIO : Quiet! You will make him angry. His love is blind.

MERCUTIO : Good night, Romeo. He is probably sitting under a tree, dreaming about that girl. He is mad.

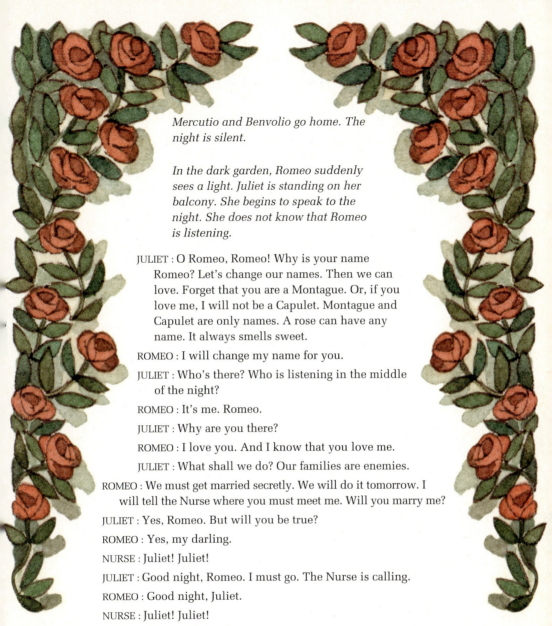

Mercutio and Benvolio go home. The night is silent.

In the dark garden, Romeo suddenly sees a light. Juliet is standing on her balcony. She begins to speak to the night. She does not know that Romeo is listening.

JULIET : O Romeo, Romeo! Why is your name Romeo? Let's change our names. Then we can love. Forget that you are a Montague. Or, if you love me, I will not be a Capulet. Montague and Capulet are only names. A rose can have any name. It always smells sweet.

ROMEO : I will change my name for you.

JULIET : Who's there? Who is listening in the middle of the night?

ROMEO : It's me. Romeo.

JULIET : Why are you there?

ROMEO : I love you. And I know that you love me.

JULIET : What shall we do? Our families are enemies.

ROMEO : We must get married secretly. We will do it tomorrow. I will tell the Nurse where you must meet me. Will you marry me?

JULIET : Yes, Romeo. But will you be true?

ROMEO : Yes, my darling.

NURSE : Juliet! Juliet!

JULIET : Good night, Romeo. I must go. The Nurse is calling.

ROMEO : Good night, Juliet.

NURSE : Juliet! Juliet!

JULIET : I'm coming, Nurse. Good night.

ROMEO : Good night.

JULIET : Good night.

ROMEO : *(further away)* Good night.

JULIET : It is very sad and very sweet to say good night. But tomorrow, we will be married.

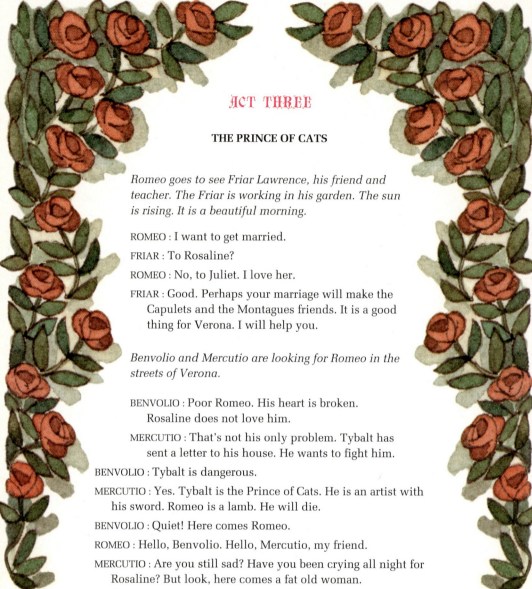

ACT THREE

THE PRINCE OF CATS

Romeo goes to see Friar Lawrence, his friend and teacher. The Friar is working in his garden. The sun is rising. It is a beautiful morning.

ROMEO : I want to get married.

FRIAR : To Rosaline?

ROMEO : No, to Juliet. I love her.

FRIAR : Good. Perhaps your marriage will make the Capulets and the Montagues friends. It is a good thing for Verona. I will help you.

Benvolio and Mercutio are looking for Romeo in the streets of Verona.

BENVOLIO : Poor Romeo. His heart is broken. Rosaline does not love him.

MERCUTIO : That's not his only problem. Tybalt has sent a letter to his house. He wants to fight him.

BENVOLIO : Tybalt is dangerous.

MERCUTIO : Yes. Tybalt is the Prince of Cats. He is an artist with his sword. Romeo is a lamb. He will die.

BENVOLIO : Quiet! Here comes Romeo.

ROMEO : Hello, Benvolio. Hello, Mercutio, my friend.

MERCUTIO : Are you still sad? Have you been crying all night for Rosaline? But look, here comes a fat old woman.

NURSE : Romeo, Romeo. I must talk with you, privately. Do you have any news for Juliet?

ROMEO : Yes. Tell Juliet to come to Friar Lawrence's cell this afternoon. We will get married there.

NURSE : I love Juliet, sir. I remember when she was a little child. Look after her when you are her husband.

The Nurse goes back to Juliet. She tells her the news. The two lovers get ready for their secret wedding. In the afternoon, the sun is shining. Romeo goes secretly to Friar Lawrence's cell.

FRIAR: The day is bright. It is a sign that the future will be happy.

ROMEO: I do not care if I die tomorrow. It is enough that Juliet is mine.

FRIAR: Don't be so passionate. It is better to love moderately. Then love will last longer.

At last Juliet arrives. She is very nervous. So is Romeo. They are very young but very much in love. Friar Lawrence is like a father to them. He takes them into his cell and they are married.

But in the streets of Verona, there are problems.

TYBALT: Mercutio, where is Romeo?

MERCUTIO: I don't know. Why?

TYBALT: I want to kill him. He came to the party of the Capulets. You are his friend. You came with him. I want to fight you too.

MERCUTIO: Here is Romeo.

TYBALT: Fight, you villain!

ROMEO: I cannot fight you.

MERCUTIO: Romeo! Are you a coward? Tybalt!

TYBALT: What do you want?

MERCUTIO: I want one of your nine lives, Prince of Cats!

TYBALT: I will fight you as Romeo is too afraid to fight.

ROMEO: Stop fighting. The Prince will be angry. He will punish you. Stop, Tybalt. Stop, good Mercutio!

MERCUTIO: Aaaaagh! I am hurt. I am dying. Romeo, this quarrel between your families has killed me.

Mercutio falls to the ground and dies. It is Romeo's fault. His friend is dead.

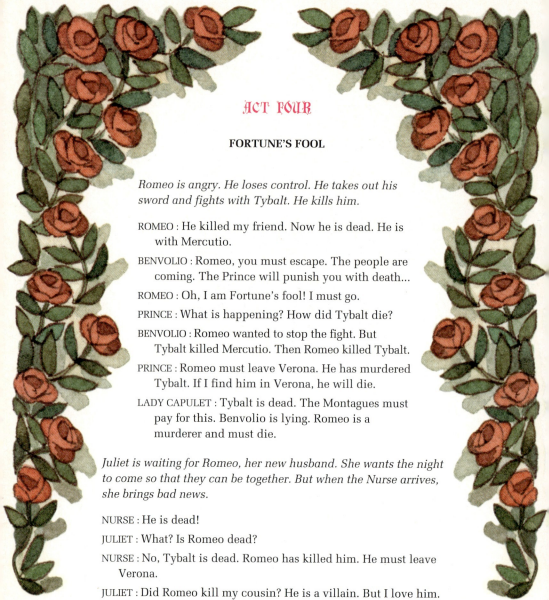

ACT FOUR

FORTUNE'S FOOL

Romeo is angry. He loses control. He takes out his sword and fights with Tybalt. He kills him.

ROMEO : He killed my friend. Now he is dead. He is with Mercutio.

BENVOLIO : Romeo, you must escape. The people are coming. The Prince will punish you with death...

ROMEO : Oh, I am Fortune's fool! I must go.

PRINCE : What is happening? How did Tybalt die?

BENVOLIO : Romeo wanted to stop the fight. But Tybalt killed Mercutio. Then Romeo killed Tybalt.

PRINCE : Romeo must leave Verona. He has murdered Tybalt. If I find him in Verona, he will die.

LADY CAPULET : Tybalt is dead. The Montagues must pay for this. Benvolio is lying. Romeo is a murderer and must die.

Juliet is waiting for Romeo, her new husband. She wants the night to come so that they can be together. But when the Nurse arrives, she brings bad news.

NURSE : He is dead!

JULIET : What? Is Romeo dead?

NURSE : No, Tybalt is dead. Romeo has killed him. He must leave Verona.

JULIET : Did Romeo kill my cousin? He is a villain. But I love him.

NURSE : Your father and mother are crying for Tybalt.

JULIET : I will cry for him too. But I will cry longer for Romeo. I will never see him again. I will kill myself.

NURSE : No. Romeo is hiding with Friar Lawrence. I will bring him to you.

The Nurse comes to find Romeo. He is talking to Friar Lawrence.

ROMEO : Everything is finished. I will kill myself with this knife.

FRIAR : No, be brave. You must go to Mantua. You will be safe there. I will send you news about Juliet. One day, you will be together again. But tonight, go with the Nurse. See Juliet for the last time.

NURSE : Come with me. Here is the house of the Capulets. Here is a ladder. Climb up and go through the window.

So Romeo spends his marriage night with Juliet.

Downstairs, in the house of the Capulets, Lord and Lady Capulet are talking. Lord Paris is with them.

LORD CAPULET : I will talk to Juliet. She will marry you next Thursday. Tybalt is dead. There must be something good for the Capulet family – Juliet's wedding! I am her father. She will do as I say. Wife, see Juliet in the morning and tell her. She will marry Paris.

In the morning, Romeo leaves Juliet. He must escape to Mantua before the Prince finds him.

JULIET : Must you go? It is still night. The nightingale is singing, not the lark.

ROMEO : Look at the sky. The sun is rising. But I want to stay.

JULIET : Go. It is dangerous for you here. But I want you to stay. Goodbye, sweet Romeo. Will I ever see you again?

ROMEO : Goodbye. I will think of you every second of the day.

ACT FIVE

MY LADY'S DEAD!

Lady Capulet tells Juliet that she must marry Paris.

LADY CAPULET : You will get married to Paris early next Thursday morning.

JULIET : No, Mother. As you know, I hate Romeo. He has killed my cousin. But I'd rather marry Romeo than Paris.

JULIET *(thinking)* : I am already married.

LORD CAPULET : Paris is a fine gentleman. Marry him on Thursday or never speak to me again.

NURSE : Please don't be angry with my little Juliet, sir.

LORD CAPULET : Shut up, you fat old fool. I have decided. If you don't obey me, I will throw you out in the streets. Goodbye. Remember, on Thursday, you are going to be married.

LADY CAPULET : Goodbye, daughter. You must obey your father.

JULIET : Nurse, tell me, what should I do?

NURSE : Well, Romeo is not here. Paris is a fine gentleman, it's true. He is more handsome than Romeo. Forget Romeo and marry Paris.

JULIET : Do you speak from your heart?*(thinking)* I cannot trust her. I will ask the Friar for advice. He is the only person who can help me.

The Friar is very worried. He is talking to Paris.

PARIS : I am going to marry Juliet.

FRIAR : Does she love you?

PARIS : I don't know. We haven't talked about love because she is weeping for her cousin's death. But our marriage will make her happy again.

FRIAR : But look, here comes Juliet.

PARIS: Welcome, my lady and my wife. Have you come to tell the Friar that you love me?

JULIET: I cannot answer that. But please, let me talk to the Friar privately.

PARIS: Goodbye. I know that you love me. I will see you on Thursday in the church.

FRIAR: Be happy, Juliet. I have a plan. You and Romeo will be together.

JULIET: Tell me! What is it?

FRIAR: Go home and agree to marry Paris. On Wednesday night, go to your bedroom alone. Take this bottle and drink the liquid. It is a special potion. You will sleep for forty-two hours. Your family will think that you are dead. They will carry you to the tomb of the Capulets. Meanwhile, I will send a message to Romeo. He will come secretly to the tomb. When you wake up, you can escape together. Are you brave enough to do this, Juliet?

JULIET: Give me the bottle, Friar. Love will give me strength.

Juliet goes home.

JULIET: Mother, Father, I have changed my mind. I will obey you. I have seen Lord Paris at the Friar's cell and I've told him that I love him.

LORD CAPULET: Good, you are a good daughter.

LADY CAPULET: You have made your old father happy.

JULIET: Now I am going to my room to pray. Do not come with me, Nurse, I want to be alone.

PAUSE

JULIET: Here is the bottle. I am afraid. Perhaps it is poison. Or perhaps I will wake in the tomb and Romeo will not be there. I will be alone in the middle of all the dead bodies with my dead cousin, Tybalt. It will be terrible.

Bravely, Juliet picks up the bottle and raises it to her lips.

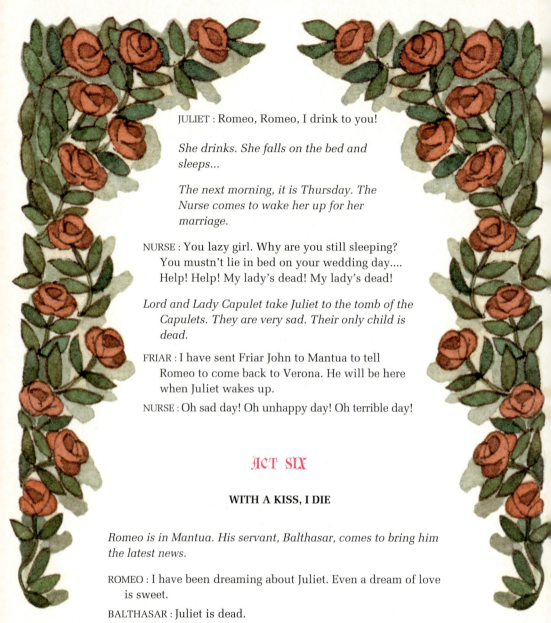

JULIET : Romeo, Romeo, I drink to you!

She drinks. She falls on the bed and sleeps...

The next morning, it is Thursday. The Nurse comes to wake her up for her marriage.

NURSE : You lazy girl. Why are you still sleeping? You mustn't lie in bed on your wedding day.... Help! Help! My lady's dead! My lady's dead!

Lord and Lady Capulet take Juliet to the tomb of the Capulets. They are very sad. Their only child is dead.

FRIAR : I have sent Friar John to Mantua to tell Romeo to come back to Verona. He will be here when Juliet wakes up.

NURSE : Oh sad day! Oh unhappy day! Oh terrible day!

ACT SIX

WITH A KISS, I DIE

Romeo is in Mantua. His servant, Balthasar, comes to bring him the latest news.

ROMEO : I have been dreaming about Juliet. Even a dream of love is sweet.

BALTHASAR : Juliet is dead.

ROMEO : What! I will ride to Verona tonight. I will kiss her for the last time. Then I will drink poison. If Juliet is dead, I will die too.

In the middle of the night, Romeo arrives at the tomb of the Capulets. Paris is also there with his servant.

PARIS : I have come to put flowers on Juliet's grave. But who is this? You are a Montague, the one who killed Tybalt. You must die.

ROMEO: I do not know you. Go away if you want to live. Do not fight with me. I am desperate. I am stronger than tigers or the roaring sea.

PARIS: I arrest you, murderer.
They fight.

ROMEO: It is Paris! I have killed him. Balthasar told me that he wanted to marry Juliet. We are both unlucky. But where is Juliet? I must look at her beauty for the last time.

PAUSE

ROMEO: Oh my love, my wife! Death has kissed you. But you are still beautiful. Death is jealous. He keeps you here as his lover. I will also stay here. But let me kiss you. With a kiss, I die.

Romeo kisses Juliet. He takes a cup of poison out of his pocket and raises it to his lips.

FRIAR: Romeo! Romeo!

Friar John has come to Friar Lawrence's cell.

FRIAR: Have you given my letter to Romeo, Friar John?

JOHN: No, Friar Lawrence. I did not reach Mantua. There was plague in one of the villages on the road and the soldiers did not let me pass.

FRIAR: What! This is bad news. If Juliet wakes when Romeo is not there, she will be afraid. I must go to her.

PAUSE

FRIAR: I can see a light in the tomb. Who is looking among the skulls and the worms?
BALTHASAR: It is my master, Romeo.
FRIAR: I must go to him. Romeo! Romeo!

But when the Friar goes inside the tomb, Romeo has already drunk the poison. He is dead.

Juliet wakes up and sees the Friar.

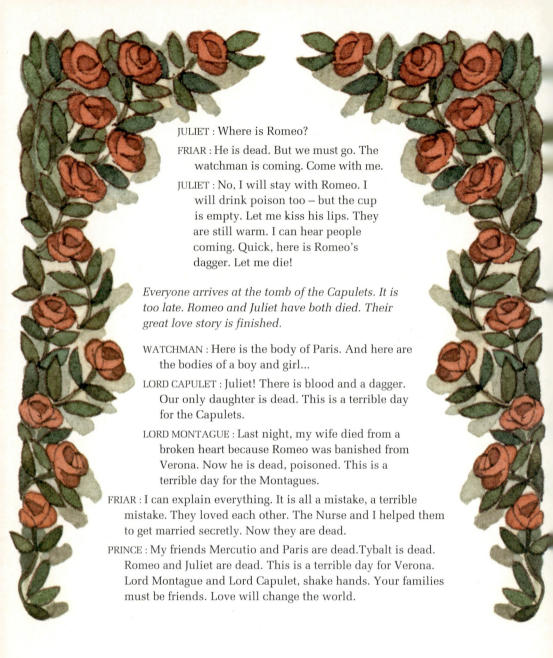

JULIET : Where is Romeo?

FRIAR : He is dead. But we must go. The watchman is coming. Come with me.

JULIET : No, I will stay with Romeo. I will drink poison too – but the cup is empty. Let me kiss his lips. They are still warm. I can hear people coming. Quick, here is Romeo's dagger. Let me die!

Everyone arrives at the tomb of the Capulets. It is too late. Romeo and Juliet have both died. Their great love story is finished.

WATCHMAN : Here is the body of Paris. And here are the bodies of a boy and girl...

LORD CAPULET : Juliet! There is blood and a dagger. Our only daughter is dead. This is a terrible day for the Capulets.

LORD MONTAGUE : Last night, my wife died from a broken heart because Romeo was banished from Verona. Now he is dead, poisoned. This is a terrible day for the Montagues.

FRIAR : I can explain everything. It is all a mistake, a terrible mistake. They loved each other. The Nurse and I helped them to get married secretly. Now they are dead.

PRINCE : My friends Mercutio and Paris are dead. Tybalt is dead. Romeo and Juliet are dead. This is a terrible day for Verona. Lord Montague and Lord Capulet, shake hands. Your families must be friends. Love will change the world.

987 654 3